'It is now widely recognised that older adults should have access to a range of evidence-based interventions for depression and low mood. Professor Williams and colleagues have been at the forefront of advocating and developing effective tools to achieve this. The resources here provide staff and individuals direct access to expert-written life skills resources that can allow older adults to learn effective strategies they can use to make changes that can quite literally be life changing. *Overcoming Depression and Low Mood in Older Adults* provides a wide suite of resources that address all the most common areas of need of older adults and their carers. I warmly welcome and highly recommend this excellent set of resources.'

Stephen Curran, BSc (Hons), MB ChB, MMedSc, MRCPsych, PhD, *Professor, trained in Leeds and was a Lecturer in old age psychiatry at the University of Leeds until he took up his current post as Consultant in old age psychiatry in Wakefield, UK. He has published many peer-reviewed publications and nearly 20 books on depression, dementia and psychopharmacology in older people and more recently on medical management for doctors. He is a co-author of* Practical Psychiatry of Old Age *(5th Edition).*

T0373524

Overcoming Depression and Low Mood in Older Adults

Overcoming Depression and Low Mood in Older Adults joins the bestselling Routledge *Overcoming Series*, which includes publications that have the seal of approval from the Association for Behavioral and Cognitive Therapies and are highly commended by the British Medical Association.

This workbook outlines how to use the Five Areas® model of cognitive behavioural therapy (CBT) to equip older adults experiencing low mood or depression with key life skills to overcome these conditions.

Addressing the common challenges faced by older adults during times of low mood and depression, the book provides educational life skills and resources to increase mental well-being in the care home, day hospital and social support networks of this population. Chapters cover topics such as understanding and changing behaviours; behavioural activation and tackling avoidance; noticing and changing extreme and unhelpful thoughts; rebalancing relationships; building assertiveness; and problem solving. Substantially featured throughout are worksheet resources using interactive questions that can be photocopied for use by practitioners with older and workbook adults or in their routine business as a therapist or health/social care practitioner.

This is a valuable text for any healthcare or mental health professional working with older adults including psychological therapists, social care workers, residential home staff, psychiatrists and practice nurses, general practitioners and health visiting staff. The workbook is also an approachable resource for older adults themselves.

Award-winning author Professor **Chris Williams** is an Emeritus Professor of Psychiatry at the University of Glasgow, UK, and an Honorary Fellow and Past President of BABCP – the lead body for CBT in the UK. He is a well-known writer, teacher and researcher and his work focuses on making CBT approaches accessible and usable. He is also Director of Five Areas Ltd which produces a range of written and online CBT based resources for use across the lifespan. Discover more at www.llttf.com/evidence

Overcoming Series

Series Editor: Chris Williams

The Overcoming series uses the tried and tested Five Areas® model of CBT to equip and empower readers with the key life skills they need to overcome the challenges these conditions present.

The Five Areas® model communicates life skills and key interventions in a clear, pragmatic, and accessible style, by examining five important aspects of our lives:

- Life situation, relationships, practical resources and problems

- Altered thinking

- Altered feelings or moods

- Altered physical symptoms or sensations

- Altered behaviour or activity levels

Titles in the series:

Overcoming Teenage Low Mood and Depression
Nicky Dummett & Chris Williams

Overcoming Postnatal Depression
Chris Williams, Roch Cantwell and Karen Robertson

Overcoming Anxiety, Stress and Panic, Third Edition
Chris Williams

Overcoming Depression and Low Mood, Fourth Edition
Chris Williams

Overcoming Teenage Low Mood and Depression, Second Edition
Nicky Dummett & Chris Williams

Overcoming Depression and Low Mood in Older Adults: A Five Areas® CBT Approach
Chris Williams

For further information about this series please visit:
https://www.routledge.com/Overcoming/book-series/CRCOVERCOMIN

Overcoming Depression and Low Mood in Older Adults

A Five Areas® CBT Approach

Chris Williams

Routledge
Taylor & Francis Group

LONDON AND NEW YORK

First published 2024
by Routledge
4 Park Square, Milton Park, Abingdon, Oxon OX14 4RN

and by Routledge
605 Third Avenue, New York, NY 10158

Routledge is an imprint of the Taylor & Francis Group, an informa business

British Library Cataloguing-in-Publication Data
A catalogue record for this book is available from the British Library

Library of Congress Cataloging-in-Publication Data
Names: Williams, Chris, 1964- author.
Title: Overcoming depression and low mood in older adults : a five areas CBT approach / Chris Williams.
Description: Abingdon, Oxon ; New York, NY : Routledge, 2024. |
Series: Overcoming series | Includes index. |
Identifiers: LCCN 2023037715 (print) | LCCN 2023037716 (ebook) |
ISBN 9781032389455 (hbk) | ISBN 9781032389448 (pbk) |
ISBN 9781003347637 (ebk)
Subjects: LCSH: Depression in old age--Treatment. | Cognitive therapy.
Classification: LCC RC537.5 .W55 2024 (print) | LCC RC537.5 (ebook) |
DDC 618.97/68527--dc23/eng/20231018
LC record available at https://lccn.loc.gov/2023037715
LC ebook record available at https://lccn.loc.gov/2023037716

ISBN: 978-1-032-38945-5 (hbk)
ISBN: 978-1-032-38944-8 (pbk)
ISBN: 978-1-003-34763-7 (ebk)

DOI: 10.4324/9781003347637

Typeset in Frutiger
by KnowledgeWorks Global Ltd.

Contents

Part 6: Planning for the future

Introduction

Overcoming depression and low mood in older adults is written for two main groups of people:

1 Older adults themselves, who are struggling with low mood or low mood and anxiety.

2 Practitioners such as doctors, nurses, mental health or social care-based workers, who are looking for high-quality resources that they can use with older adults they work with.

About the resources

This book is one of a range of resources created by Five Areas Resources Ltd, and made available under licence by Five Areas Ltd. It uses the widely recommended CBT approach. This book is one of a series of books in the Overcoming … Five Areas® series. The companion book *Overcoming depression and low mood: a five areas® approach* is aimed at adult readers. This book has been widely recommended. It has been recognised and highly recommended by the British Medical Association (BMA) Medical Book awards and has received the Self-help Seal of Approval by the Association for Behavioural and Cognitive Therapies (ABCT: https://www.abct.org/sh-books/)

Read research about that book and the evidence base supporting its use at: www.llttf.com/evidence

About the author

Professor Chris Williams is a medical doctor and an Emeritus Professor of Psychosocial Psychiatry at the University of Glasgow. His first degree was in Psychology in relation to medicine, and his subsequent work has focused on how to widen how to widen access to evidence-based psychological therapies. His main research and teaching focus has been on how to create CBT-based resources that are usable, and effective. He has written over 40 books, and over a million copies of his titles have been sold worldwide. His award-winning books have been translated into over 15 languages. He has also twice been President of the lead body for CBT in the UK – the British Association for Behavioural and Cognitive Psychotherapies (BABCP www.babcp.com).

Professor Williams is also the Director of Five Areas Limited (www.fiveareas.com) which develops and publishes a range of books, online courses and practitioner class resources for use in educational and health, charity and social care settings.

How this book can be used

This book is based on the widely used and recommended *Overcoming depression and low mood: a five areas®* approach book – for adults. It has been updated by specialist workers with older adults/seniors in Oregon who commissioned a re-write of the book for older adults to be used Statewide in the State of Oregon USA. This work was led by North-West Senior and Disability Services (https://nwsds.org/), a local intergovernmental agency serving seniors and adults with physical disabilities in five Oregon counties. The book is made available with peer mentor support as part of the Healthy Opportunities for Personal Empowerment (HOPE) Senior Peer Mentor Program. Senior Peer Mentors are volunteers (age 45 or older) who are trained and supervised. The HOPE Senior Peer Mentor Program is free. It is aimed at older adults aged 50 or older who wish to gain more effective coping skills to help manage their mild to moderate depression and/or anxiety.

The current version of this book has been updated again by Professor Williams and colleagues Mrs Theresa Kelly, and Mrs Sue Wood, to provide an up-to-date well-being resource for older adults.

The book can be read in order but is usually used by picking out the content that is relevant.

Recommended reading

Read Part 1 of the book:

a *Starting out … and how to keep going if you feel stuck*

b *Understanding why you feel as you do*

This will help you identify which other workbooks might be useful for you to work through.

Then select what topics and chapters might be relevant from Parts 2 and 3 of the book. Additional optional topics are held in Part 4 of the book. Finally, there is a summary/review of learning in the final Part of the book which addresses *Planning for the future*.

The reader can work through as few or as many workbooks as they find useful. Typically, many readers will read the opening two chapters, then 3–5 additional topics.

You can use the workbooks as *self-directed learning* by yourself.

Or use it with *support from a supporter or practitioner*. Here, we recommend that the relationship is one of tutor/trainer/coach, helping readers choose what topics they wish to work on, clarifying understanding by asking questions, and applying and discussing what you are learning.

Practitioner Training: We offer Practitioner training for health and social are workers, as well as businesses/self-employed practitioners via www.llttf.com/training

Foreword

Depression in older adults has been poorly recognised and often either overlooked – or misidentified as part of getting old. That is misleading because depression is common in older adults – with 1:10 affected.

Depression and low mood in older people are often also associated with poor physical health such as hearing loss, poor sight, chronic pain, thyroid disease, cancer and/or disability. Older adulthood is also a time of changes and often of losses. Losses of job role with retirement can be also key. Sometimes people can become distanced and socially isolated from friends and family as they grow older, - perhaps because they find it more difficult to get out and about or travel on their own. Losses become more frequent as we age and get older. This can not only be the loss of family members, partners or friends but can also be due to the loss of health, pets or even losing their home due to life changes.

It is now widely recognised that older adults should have access to a range of evidence-based interventions for depression and low mood. Part of the challenge for services to offer support for older adults is a significant mismatch between the large demand for treatment, and the lack of resources to achieve this. Part of the solution is the low-intensity revolution with the recognition that access to CBT-based treatments and supports can be offered using books, websites and classes – as well as the traditional route of seeing an accredited, expert CBT practitioner.

Professor Williams and colleagues have been at the forefront of advocating and developing effective tools to achieve this. The resources are very widely used across the UK and internationally, and provide staff and individuals direct access to expert-written life skills resources that can allow older adults to learn effective strategies they can use to make changes that can quite literally be life-changing. *Overcoming depression and low mood in older adults* provides a wide suite of resources that address all the most common areas of need of older adults and their carers.

I warmly welcome and highly recommend this excellent set of resources.

Professor Stephen Curran, BSc (Hons), MB ChB, MMedSc, MRCPsych, PhD, trained in Leeds and was a Lecturer in old age psychiatry at the University of Leeds until he took up his current post as a Consultant in old age psychiatry in Wakefield, UK. He has published many peer view publications and nearly 20 books on depression, dementia and psychopharmacology in older people and more recently on medical management for doctors. He is a co-author of Practical Psychiatry of Old Age (5th Edition).

Acknowledgements

Photo image licenses from iStockphoto.com. The cartoon illustrations were produced by Keith Chan, kchan75@hotmail.com. Thank you to Mrs Theresa Kelly and Mrs Sue Wood at Five Areas Ltd for their helpful advice and comments on earlier drafts of this book. Also, to those practitioners and Peer mentors at North West Senior and Disability Services in Oregon, USA who inputted into the initial modifications of these resources to suit an older adult readership.

PART 1

Getting started and understanding why you feel as you do

Overcoming Depression and Low Mood in Older Adults

A Five Areas® CBT Approach

Starting out ... and how to keep going if you feel stuck

Dr Chris Williams

DOI: 10.4324/9781003347637-2

Do you ever notice this?

Are you feeling like this?

If so, … these workbooks are for you.

Welcome.

The *Overcoming depression and low mood in older adults* course consists of a series of workbooks that cover a range of issues that are often experienced by people in their later years at times when they struggle with low mood or stress. They aim to help you learn key life skills to help you improve how you feel at times of low mood or stress. Whoever you are, whatever your background life situation – these resources are written having you in mind.

In this course you will:

- Learn about the structure of the course and what content to use next.

- Discover ways of getting the most out of the course and staying motivated as you work through it.

- Find out how to make clear, flexible plans for change.

- Discover how to overcome problems that can make change difficult.

Why use these workbooks?

People use these workbooks because they want to make helpful changes to their lives.

The content is based on an approach called cognitive behavioural therapy (CBT), a kind of widely used and recommended talking therapy. Research has shown that written materials based on the CBT approach can help people overcome problems such as depression and also related problems such as anxiety. Research of this approach in adults in the UK and in the Canadian national Bounceback programme has shown that it can help readers to improve how they feel. People using the workbook often feel less depressed and more able to live their lives as they want.

The author of this book is an Emeritus Professor of Psychiatry at the University of Glasgow, Scotland, UK. Professor Williams is an internationally known expert who has spent many years working and evaluating the area of CBT. He has twice been President of the British Association for Behavioural and Cognitive Psychotherapies (www.babcp.com) – the lead body for CBT in the UK. His interest and research work have focused on ways of taking the evidence-based CBT approach and developing a wide range of formats like books, classes and online resources that people can easily access and use to improve how they feel when they are struggling with low mood or stress.

About Bounceback

In Canada, the Canadian Mental Health Association delivers these resources nationally in both English and French versions. Content has been modified to suit a Canadian setting, and made available with telephone and face-to-face coaching support.

Making changes

As we get older, it can feel harder and harder to keep doing the things we've been used to doing when younger. We may become physically less able to get going. Travelling can seem harder, whether we are driving ourselves or getting a lift. Sometimes, using public transport can be daunting, and things that at one time might have seemed easy like catching a bus, train or airplane now may seem harder or too much to face. Our lives might seem smaller as a result.

At times when we struggle, it can seem even harder to maintain what we do, and times of low mood or stress can sap our motivation even more, and change can seem too much. The workbooks and linked resources have proved helpful to many. But they won't help unless they are read and put into practice. We know that might feel difficult. But we do encourage you to give it a go and test out what happens.

What should I read first?

People usually start by working through two workbooks:

• This one – *Starting out … and how to keep going if you feel stuck.*

• And then *Understanding why you feel as you do.*

They will help you understand how your low mood is affecting you and decide which other course workbooks might help. These cover a range of content such as tackling practical problems, responding differently to unhelpful thoughts, sleeping better and maintaining activities so you live life as fully as you can.

KEY POINT

Choose the content *you* want to work on – so you deal with the problems/difficulties you are facing.

Also, think about changes you can make in the short term (this week), and medium term (over the next few weeks and months). It's not a race, small steady steps all add up.

Get into a routine

Workbooks are exactly this – a book that is worked on. It's helpful to get into a routine of using the workbooks and applying them. You might wish to set aside a particular time and place to sit down and work on your chosen topic.

Getting into the mood: doing something physical can help you get started

It's usual to feel physically and mentally sluggish when you are low or when you haven't been sleeping well. It can help you become energised to work on change if you plan a short physical activity before starting to read. For example get up and walk around the room if you can. Or (if you have them) – go up and down the stairs or do chair/arm exercises if you can't walk.

Choose a chair like a kitchen chair that is upright and forces you to sit straight rather than slump back may help.

Plan enough time so that you can get really involved in the workbook – preferably half an hour or so, if you have sufficient energy and concentration for this. If you have others around you who might interrupt or distract such as grandchildren or a partner, try to choose a time when they are not around, or ask not to be disturbed.

If you feel tired halfway through, stop, get physically going again. Stretch, have some cold water, tea, juice or coffee, then get back to work.

Getting the most out of the workbook

It can be helpful to:

- Slow it down. Focus on just one workbook at a time.

- **Get a pen and paper**. Writing things down means you are thinking and learning. In fact, it's more than that. Things can look different when we write them down. We can notice patterns and habits we might otherwise miss. Sometimes we can start to really work out what is happening when we see it on a page in black and white. Therefore, try to answer the questions right now rather than thinking you will come back to it later. You don't need to get it '*right*' or answer in great detail. Just do what you can.

  Try to answer all the questions – and *stop, think and reflect* as you read.

- **Ask:** How might I use this in my life?

- Try out and apply what you read in the workbooks. You can **download** additional blank worksheets to practice applying the skills you are learning from www.llttf.com/resources.

- **Be realistic.** You are more likely to succeed if you try changing things one step at a time rather than throwing yourself into things and then running out of steam.

- **Re-read the workbooks.** You may find that different parts become clearer or seem more useful on reading them second time.

- Use the workbooks to build on help you receive in other ways, such as talking to your doctor, health worker or coach. Or share what you're learning with friends or within any self-help organisation or support groups you attend.

- Keep the resources organised and at hand. Create your own *Resource Pack* of key worksheets and other resources you use to improve how you feel.

- Try to complete these workbooks alongside any other support recommended by your doctor or support worker such as taking prescribed anti-depressant medication. These approaches can be all helpful parts of moving forward.

It's not helpful to:

- Read through the entire book or workbook at one time. If you slow things down it gives you time to really take it in, and then apply what you're learning in practice.

- Be unrealistic in how quickly you'll feel different. Change takes time and practice.

- Try to read the workbook when you are distracted. For example times when you are juggling other tasks.

- Cut yourself off from other useful supports.

Finding extra support

Having someone around who can offer *support and encouragement* can help. This is especially important if you feel you are struggling or feel stuck. Sometimes just the act of telling someone that you are working on change, or plan to do a certain activity on a particular day can really help. Just knowing that someone else may ask you how it's going may help spur you to action.

If you're feeling isolated, think broadly who can support you. This might be someone from a health or social care team – ask your General Practitioner (GP) what is available. It's okay to ask for support. In settings such as NHS talking therapies or mental health teams in the UK or Ireland, or Bounceback in Canada, coaching or practitioner support is offered. That's a great opportunity to find encouragement and support, as well as having someone to turn to if you get stuck or have questions.

Or you could ask a family member, friend or someone supportive from your faith community (if this applies to you). Whoever you turn to for support, the key is they should be someone you can trust to share your experiences with. You might go through your answers to the questions in the workbooks with them – or keep your answers private and only discuss some of the workbook content.

Building your motivation to change

It can sometimes feel difficult knowing how to start to make changes. If you have low motivation levels, it might stop you getting very far with change. Or perhaps you're put off if something seems hard or you feel stuck? It's even more common to feel like this during times of low mood and stress.

Here is a task you can do at times when motivation seems to wane.

TASK: Imagine it is a year in the future. You have made helpful changes in your life and things are much better. Write yourself an **encouraging letter** about why you need to make changes now, and how much better you'll feel when things improve. Keep it somewhere safe and bring it out whenever you feel stuck.

Dear (your name)

Signed:
Me

Remember, change takes time and effort

Sometimes it's easy to forget how hard it is to learn new information or skills that you now take for granted. Think about some of the skills you have learned over the years. For example if you can drive, swim or ride a bike, – now think back to your first driving/swimming lesson or attempt to cycle without stabilisers. You probably weren't very good at it that first time, yet with practice you may have developed the skills needed to do it. In the same way, you can help overcome how you feel by practicing the new skills this course will teach you – even if it may seem very hard at first. We are never too old to learn.

TASK: Write down some other things you have learned that took time.

_____

_____

KEY POINT

You wouldn't expect a child to be able to swim immediately. They need to start at the shallow end and practice at first. It's the same for all the changes you make. Pace what you do and don't jump straight in at the deep end.

Be realistic

It's important not to approach this course either far too positively, or far too negatively. It would be untrue to claim that you are guaranteed results. What we can guarantee is that this approach has helped many thousands of people – and that the workbooks teach approaches that have been a help for many people. Hopefully, at the very least you will learn some interesting and helpful things along the way.

Common problems in using the workbooks: I have no time

Sometimes life is full of commitments. Perhaps supporting children, grandchildren or friends? Or looking after a poorly partner or friend, or juggling various activities and interests? It can also seem a full-time job coping with our or a close one's illness. There may be multiple appointments for treatment or investigations, the need to drop off samples, or have blood tests or more at the health centre, clinic or hospital. If so, just take the time to work on the course when you can.

TASK: Imagine you have a close friend who is struggling with low mood and stress. What helpful advice would you give them if they said 'I don't have time.' Write down your encouraging advice here:

_____

_____

If you would give your friend helpful advice to make some time – then why not offer the same advice to yourself?

I feel too down to do this now

Sometimes depression causes such poor levels of concentration and energy, that using course workbooks like these seems too much. But you can always come back to them later when you're feeling brighter. You should also discuss your treatment options with key people like your doctor, coach, your trusted family member or well-being support worker.

But … I'll never change

Perhaps the biggest block to getting better is not believing that change can happen. Many people find that they gain much more from the workbooks than they first thought they would. Could this be true for you?

TASK: What kind words of encouragement would you give a friend who needed help but believed that change is impossible? Write them down here:

_____

_____

Again, if you would be kind and compassionate to a friend, then why not do the same to yourself?

Try things out and experiment

In the workbooks, you will find you are often asked to experiment and try things out to test what happens. The aim is to discover for yourself which suggestions most help you. It also will help you look back on the growing list of skills you are learning that can make a difference.

Making plans for change

Change can sometimes be difficult. Because of this, it can help to have a written plan of **what** you will do and **when** you will do it.

 EXAMPLE:

Here's an example plan that looks at when and how to start reading the next recommended resource – *Understanding why you feel as you do.*

1   **What am I going to do?**

   Suggestion: Start to read the *Understanding why you feel as you do* workbook.

   If you decide to do this, think through in more detail exactly **what** you will do. Do you need to break it down into smaller parts? For example get a pen and paper, find a copy of the workbook, sit at the table with the door shut and turn off your TV and radio. Be realistic. Will you plan to read many pages of the workbook, or just a few pages at a time?

   Write what you will do here:

   _____

2 <u>**When**</u> **am I going to do it?**

What date and time will suit? Many people with low mood or stress notice they feel at their worst first thing in the morning. So, you might find that the best time for you to read the workbook is after lunch, in the late afternoon, or in the early evening. If you live with others, think about what you know about their routine. Do you need quiet, or do you want others around to discuss topics with? Also, can you plan to read it every day – or do you need a gap to let things sink in?

Write the day and time:_____

3 **Is my planned task:**

Ⓠ Useful for understanding or changing how I am?

  Yes ☐   No ☐

Ⓠ Clear and specific, so that I will know when I have done it?

  Yes ☐   No ☐

Ⓠ Realistic, practical and achievable?

  Yes ☐   No ☐

4 **What problems/difficulties could arise, and how can I overcome them?**

_____

_____

(helpful hint!) **Hint: What could get in the way?**

i **Things within you** – low motivation, forgetfulness, talking yourself out of it?

ii **Or things outside you** – other people, bad weather or the need for money to do an activity, having to look after a poorly grandchild with little notice? Or perhaps a task depends on someone else for success? Or perhaps unpredictable things may also happen from time to time and interrupt your plans. For example what if a friend unexpectedly drops by for a coffee?

Write possible blocks here:

_____

_____

Finally, think again about the task and decide whether you need to re-write your plan to tackle these possible blocks.

_____

_____

Now, carry out your plan

Put your plan into action.

My Review of how it went

Afterwards, stop and reflect on how things went.

- What went well?

- What didn't go so well?

- How can you take what you've learned so you make better and better plans going forward?

Now write down your own review:

_____

_____

_____

Whichever tasks and workbooks you use, keep coming back to this *Plan, Do, Review* approach. You can even use it to plan the weekly shopping! It's all about planning effective progress and learning about what works and what doesn't in your own life right now.

SUMMARY

Well done – you've got to the last part of the workbook – and you're still reading! That's a great achievement. So many people who want to change find it hard starting out.

Let's review what you have learned in this workbook. You have covered:

- How to get the most out of the workbooks;

- The need for a clear but flexible plan of when to use the workbooks; and

- How to overcome common blocks to change.

Before you go

What have you learned from this workbook?

_____

_____

What do you want to try next?

_____

_____

Here are suggested tasks to practice this approach:

- Use the Planner and Review sheets (copies at the end of the workbook) to plan what you will do next.

- We recommend you work on the *Understanding why you feel as you do* workbook next.

Worksheets to help you put what you've learned into practice

Practice is important to help you master this approach. You can get free access to additional worksheets used in this workbook chapter and the wider book at www.llttf.com/resources

Acknowledgements

The cartoon illustrations were produced by Keith Chan, kchan75@hotmail.com. Thank you to Mrs Theresa Kelly and Mrs Sue Wood at Five Areas Ltd for their helpful advice and comments on earlier drafts of this book. Also, to those practitioners and Peer mentors at North West Senior and Disability Services in Oregon, USA who inputted into the initial modifications of these resources to suit an older adult readership, and the Bounceback participants for their useful feedback. The term Five Areas® is a registered trademark of Five Areas Resources Ltd. Although we hope you find this book helpful, it's not intended to be a direct substitute for consultative advice with a healthcare professional, nor do we give any assurance about its effectiveness in a particular case. Accordingly, neither we nor the author shall be held liable for any loss or damages arising from its use.

Overcoming Depression and Low Mood in Older Adults

A Five Areas® CBT Approach

Understanding why you feel as you do

Dr Chris Williams

OVERCOMING SERIES

DOI: 10.4324/9781003347637-3

Do you ever notice this?

Is this you?

If it is ... this workbook is for you.

This workbook will help you to:

• Learn more about low mood and depression.

• Complete your own Five Areas® Assessment to identify how low mood and stress are affecting you.

• Consider possible targets for change and decide which other workbooks you want to work on.

• Learn when you should get extra help and where to go for it.

Understanding how you feel using the Five Areas® Approach

Let's start by finding out more about how your lowered mood affects five key areas of your life.

The Five Areas® are:

• Area 1: The situations, relationships and practical problems we face. This includes the **people and events** around us.

• Area 2: Our altered **thinking**. We tend to look at things in unhelpful ways when we feel distressed.

• Area 3: Our altered **feelings** (also called moods or emotions).

• Area 4: These strong emotional feelings lead to **altered physical symptoms/sensations** in our body.

• Area 5: Finally, all these other areas add up and lead to **altered behaviour or activity levels**. This includes both the helpful things we can do that make us feel better, and the unhelpful things we do, which can backfire and make us feel even worse.

 EXAMPLE: How low mood is affecting Paul's life

Let's think about how the Five Areas® Assessment can help Paul understand how he is feeling.

Area 1 – *Paul's Situation, relationship and practical problem*: Paul recently moved into a supported housing complex. He struggles to adjust to his new living situation. He isn't making friends there, and his family is only visiting rarely.

Area 2 – Paul's *altered thinking*: Paul's thoughts revolve around thinking he shouldn't have made the move. He also believes nobody likes him.

Area 3 – Paul's *altered feelings*: He feels low and lonely. Also angry at himself. He doesn't discuss his feelings with his family because he doesn't want to be a burden. Everyone else seems so busy they rarely stop and chat. He feels worthless and invisible.

Area 4 – Paul's *altered physical symptoms/sensations*: Paul lies in bed worrying and not sleeping. He feels tired as a result and is also off his food.

Area 5 – Paul's *altered behaviour/activity*: He stays in his room nearly all the time and says he can't make it when he is asked to join others for a game of cards.

Figure 2.1 shows how Paul's problems can be summarised using the Five Areas® Approach. This shows that what you **think** about a situation or problem can affect how you **feel physically and emotionally**. It also shows that this affects **what you do** (your behaviour or activity levels). Look at the arrows in Figure 2.1. Each of the Five Areas® of your life affects each other.

Read through the description of Paul again and compare what is written with the diagram summary. Each of the Five Areas® can affect each other. This is good news because making improvements to even one of the areas can potentially lead to improvements in many other

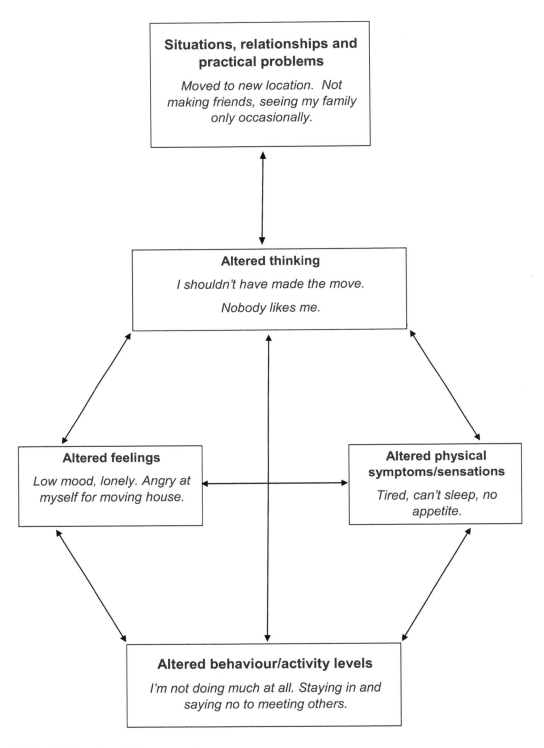

Figure 2.1 Paul's Five Areas® Assessment

areas of life as well. So, if Paul slept a bit better or made some friends, he is likely to start to notice benefits in many areas of his life.

Now complete your own Five Areas® Assessment

Now, complete your own Five Areas® Assessment. The aim is to help you understand how are feeling and also discover links between each area and determine what areas you might want to change to feel better.

Area 1: Situations, relationships and practical problems

All of us from time to time face problems caused by the people and events around us. Such as:

- Problems with family and life at home.

- The challenges of not being able to live at home.

- Problems in relationships with partners, neighbours, friends, grandchildren and caregivers.

- Other life challenges, for example reduced mobility, not being able to do activities you could previously do or making new social contacts.

Checklist: Are any of these relevant to you?

Situations, relationship or practical problem	Do you ever face these problems? (Put a check in the box if these problems are present in your life – even if just sometimes.)
There is no one around who I can really talk to.	☐
I am struggling to cope with life changes.	☐
I worry about money or debts.	☐
There are problems where I live/housing problems.	☐
It's hard to get on with another person or people in my family.	☐
I am having problems with my neighbours.	☐
I have problems with other residents.	☐
My family has unemployment/job worries.	☐
My family has housing problems.	☐
I am losing independence (e.g. can't get out by yourself or travel as far).	☐

Now write down any other difficult situations or problems you may have here:

_____

_____

_____

SUMMARY FOR AREA 1: SITUATIONS/RELATIONSHIPS/PRACTICAL PROBLEMS

Having answered the questions, rate the extent of your problems

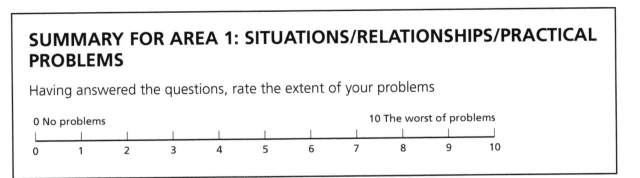

Area 2: Your altered thinking

When someone feels low or stressed, how they think tends to change. They may lose confidence and find it harder to make decisions. They may worry about things they have done – and things they haven't done. They may begin to see everything in quite anxious or negative ways and fall into negative habits of thinking.

The result is that their thinking **becomes unhelpful** and worsens how they feel.

 EXAMPLE: How Selma thinks can affect how she feels.

Selma is the caregiver for her spouse who has gradually increasing dementia. She needs to go shopping, but her spouse refuses to stay with anyone else. They become verbally abusive to the sitter. Selma cannot distract them and nothing works. She begins to feel trapped, embarrassed, and ashamed. She feels physically sick, then becomes angry and yells at her spouse that they won't let her do anything!

At times of low mood or stress it's easy for people to fall into one of several common patterns of unhelpful thinking.

The seven unhelpful thinking styles

Unhelpful thinking style	Put a check in the box if you have noticed this thinking style – even if just sometimes. Write down an example if you can.
1. *Being your own worst critic/bias against yourself.* Being very self-critical overlooking your strengths or not recognising your achievements.	☐
2. *Putting a negative slant on things* (negative mental filter). Seeing things through dark-tinted glasses; seeing the glass as being half empty rather than half full; that whatever you do in the week it's never enough; focusing on the bad side of everyday situations.	☐
3. *Having a gloomy view of the future.* Thinking that things will stay bad or get even worse; predicting that things will go wrong or always looking for the next thing to fail.	☐

4. *Jumping to the worst conclusion.* Predicting that the very worst outcome will happen; thinking that you will fail very badly.	☐
5. *Having a negative view about how others see you (mind-reading).* Often thinking that others don't like you or think badly of you for no particular reason.	☐
6. *Unfairly taking responsibility for things.* Thinking you should take the blame if things go wrong; feeling guilty about things that are not really your fault and believing that you are responsible for everyone else.	☐
7. *Making extreme statements/rules.* Using the words *'always'*, *'never'* a lot to summarise things; if a bad thing happens, saying *'Just typical'* because it seems this always happens or making yourself a lot of *'must'*, *'should'* *'ought'* or *'got to'* rules.	☐

🔑 KEY POINT

At times of low mood/stress we are more prone to think in these ways, and it's harder to put thoughts like these out of mind. These styles of thinking are called unhelpful because they have an **unhelpful impact on how we feel** (making us feel worse - low, anxious, angry, ashamed, guilty etc.) and also on **what we do** (e.g. staying inside, pushing others away etc.).

SUMMARY FOR AREA 2: ALTERED THINKING WITH UNHELPFUL THINKING PATTERNS

Having answered the questions, rate the extent of your problems

0 No problems   10 The worst of problems

```
0    1    2    3    4    5    6    7    8    9    10
```

Area 3: Your feelings/emotions

What emotional changes have you noticed over the past two weeks?	Put a check in the box if you are affected by these emotions – even if just sometimes. Write down an example if you can.
Lowness or sadness.	☐
Reduced or no sense of pleasure in things.	☐
Loss of all feelings, for example noticing no feelings at all.	☐
Guilt.	☐

(continued)

What emotional changes have you noticed over the past two weeks?	Put a check in the box if you are affected by these emotions – even if just sometimes. Write down an example if you can.
Anxiety or panic (e.g. worried, stressed, tense).	☐
Anger or irritability.	☐
Shame or embarrassment.	☐
Other (write down here):	☐

SUMMARY FOR AREA 3: ALTERED FEELINGS

Having answered the questions, rate the extent of your problems

0 No problems   10 The worst of problems

0   1   2   3   4   5   6   7   8   9   10

Area 4: Altered physical symptoms/sensations

Usually, when people feel very low emotionally, it affects how they feel physically as well.

Which physical symptoms have you noticed over the past two weeks?

Which altered physical sensations have you noticed?	Put a check in the box if you have noticed these sensations – even if just sometimes. Write down an example if you can.
Are you waking up earlier than usual?	☐
Are you finding it hard getting to sleep?	☐
Are you waking up at night or finding it hard to drop off to sleep?	☐
Has your appetite increased or decreased?	☐
Have you put on or lost weight?	☐
Do you feel as if you don't have enough energy to do things?	☐
If this affects you, have you stopped having sex or aren't interested as much in it as before?	☐
Are you constipated?	☐
Do you feel any pain?	☐
Do you feel restless?	☐
Do you have any other physical symptoms or problems such as physical illness?	☐
Write them down here:	☐

SUMMARY FOR AREA 4: ALTERED PHYSICAL SYMPTOMS

Having answered the questions, rate the extent of your problems

0 No problems   10 The worst of problems

| 0 | 1 | 2 | 3 | 4 | 5 | 6 | 7 | 8 | 9 | 10 |

Area 5: Altered behaviour or activity levels

You have already looked at the first four of the areas in your Five Areas® Assessment. Next, we look at the final area – altered behaviour (activities that you do or reduce/stop doing because of how you feel).

Many ways in which you respond can be very helpful and improve how you feel. However, some things you do can worsen how you feel, such as:

- *Reducing* your activity levels by not doing as much as before;

- *Avoiding* or escaping from doing things that seem scary or too difficult and

- Starting to respond in *unhelpful ways* that *backfire* and make you feel worse. For example by pushing others away, losing your temper at others for no good reason or having too much alcohol to block how you feel.

KEY POINT

Making changes in your behaviour and activity levels are some of the most helpful things you can do to improve how you feel.

A The vicious cycle of reduced activity

When you feel low in mood, it's often hard to keep up with things because you experience:

- Low energy and poor sleep (*'I'm too tired'*);

- Little sense of enjoyment or achievement when you do things;

- Negative thoughts and predictions about things (*'I just can't be bothered'/'I won't enjoy it'*) and....

- Everything can seem just too much, so it feels such a relief to do less.

All these lead to reduced activity. Often, we will focus our reduced energies on things we must/should/ought to do – such as helping looking after a spouse or grandchildren. Instead, the first things to be cut down or removed from life are things that have previously given you a sense of **fun/pleasure** or **achievement** (e.g. meeting up with friends and doing things with your family). You can also lose your sense of closeness/connection to others.

But *the less you do, the worse you feel, and the worse you feel, the less you do* – so a vicious cycle is set up.

Write down any examples of activities you have reduced or stopped completely here:

_____

_____

The good news is that once you have noticed whether this is true for you, you can start to plan to do these activities again.

 KEY POINT

To feel better it's not just about doing more activities in general. It's about specifically doing more of the things that give you pleasure, achievement or closeness.

You will find out more about how to do this in the _Doing things that make you feel better_ workbook

B **The vicious cycle of avoidance**

We often choose to avoid people, places and situations that make us anxious. This may make us feel better in the short-term and this explains why it's so easy to fall into cycles of doing less and less. But in the longer-term, avoiding things makes it harder and harder to confidently face our fears in the future. And we don't get to realise that our worst fears don't actually occur.

 KEY POINT

Avoidance makes you feel worse and worse, sapping your confidence and teaching you the unhelpful rule that _you only coped with a situation by avoiding it._

Write down any examples of avoidance you do here:

_____

_____

The good news is that once you have noticed if this is true for you, you can start working on tackling avoidance and facing your fears.

C **The vicious cycle of unhelpful behaviours**

Sometimes you may do things that make you feel better at first, but in the longer-term backfire and make you feel worse. Do you do any of the following unhelpful behaviours?

- Taking risks such as gambling with money you don't really have or driving when you are a risk to others?

- Pushing supporters away – for example friends or family or people from your faith community?

- Neglecting yourself (e.g. by not eating as much or not washing)?

- Taking frustrations out on others. For example by being rude, critical or 'difficult' towards others?

- Drinking excessively or misusing prescribed or non-prescribed medication?

- Harming yourself or taking unnecessary risks as a way of blocking how you feel?

Write down any examples of unhelpful behaviour you do here:

_____

_____

You can find out more about reducing unhelpful behaviours in the workbook, *Unhelpful things you do*.

SUMMARY FOR AREA 5: ANY ALTERED BEHAVIOURS OR ACTIVITY LEVELS

Now think about all the altered behaviours you have identified and rate the extent of your problems in this area.

0 No problems   10 The worst of problems

| 0 | 1 | 2 | 3 | 4 | 5 | 6 | 7 | 8 | 9 | 10 |

What next?

Remember that the purpose of the Five Areas® Approach is to help you work out how your life is being affected by your symptoms. It can help you plan the areas you need to focus on to bring about change.

The good news is that all Five Areas® are linked so making helpful changes in any one area can also lead to helpful changes in others. So, if you try to alter any one of these areas by working through a workbook targeting changes in that area, it can often help you feel better in other areas of life as well.

Where do you start?

KEY POINT

One key to successful change is to try not to tackle everything at once.

You are more likely to improve if you take slow steady steps than if you are too enthusiastic at the start and then run out of steam. So, try to take things one step at a time by choosing the topics you are going to focus on to start with.

Set yourself:

- *Short-term* targets: these are changes you can make today, tomorrow and next week.

- *Medium-term* targets: these are changes to be put in place over the next few weeks.

- *Long-term* targets: this is where you want to be in six months or a year.

Which workbook should you try first?

Your Five Areas® Assessment will help you select which workbooks to read first. Pick just one area and one workbook first. Because each of the Five Areas® affects each other, choosing any of the areas to start on makes sense. Just choose something **you** want to work on.

If you want help in deciding where to start, we recommend you read the workbooks in this order:

- The *Doing things that improve how you feel* workbook can help you quickly set a pattern to your day and plan activities that will make you feel better.

- If you are sleeping poorly, use the *Overcoming sleep problems* workbook.

- If you are taking or thinking of taking an anti-depressant try reading the workbook called *Understanding and using anti-depressant medication*.

If you have a close family member or friend you'd like to help you in using the workbook, ask them to read the *Information for families and friends* workbook. You also may find it helpful.

KEY POINT

There is no such thing as a set 'path' in this approach. The path is as many or as few workbooks as you feel you need to use. Choose ones that address topics important to you.

Check which workbooks you want to read in the table below. Place a * by the **first** workbook you intend to work on.

Workbooks	Plan to read	Check when completed
Introduction and working out what to focus on changing		
Starting out – and how to keep going if you feel stuck	☐	☐
Understanding why you feel as you do	☐	☐
Making changes to do with situations, relationships and practical problems.		
Practical problem solving	☐	☐
Being assertive	☐	☐
Building relationships with your family and friends	☐	☐
Information for families and friends – how can you offer the best support	☐	☐

Making changes to behaviours and activity levels		
Doing things that improve how you feel	☐	☐
Using exercise to improve how you feel	☐	☐
Helpful things you can do	☐	☐
Unhelpful things you do	☐	☐
Making changes to negative and upsetting thinking		
Noticing unhelpful thinking	☐	☐
Changing unhelpful thinking	☐	☐
Making changes to things that affect your physical well-being		
Overcoming sleep problems	☐	☐
Harmful drinking and you	☐	☐
Understanding and taking anti-depressant medication	☐	☐
Making changes for the future		
Planning for the future	☐	☐

KEY POINT

Repeat your Five Areas® Assessment after using each workbook to help you decide what to work on next.

How do I know if I need extra help?

If you struggle to do the tasks in the workbooks don't worry. Just do what you can. But if you feel stuck or are needing extra help, talk to your GP or health worker for advice about what other supports, treatments or inputs might be helpful.

If you have somebody supporting you, discuss what you have been doing with them.

You especially **need** to get extra help for:

- **Severe depression**, for example continuing low mood, tearfulness, not eating or drinking much at all, or a big loss of weight, despite attempts to improve things.

- Strong urges to **self-harm** or feeling really **hopeless or suicidal** about the future.

- Urges or threats to harm anyone else.

- Other **dangerous behaviours**, for example risk-taking.

- Not being able to cope so much that others around you are concerned for your health and well-being.

- Severe withdrawal from life activities.

Getting extra help

You can ask:

- **Someone you can trust** – or you may find it easier to talk to someone outside your closest friends and family. Don't feel guilty if this is the case, many people feel like this.

- **Your doctor.** He or she can give you medical advice, and (if they feel it is necessary) refer you to a specialist mental health worker or team for a full assessment.

SUMMARY

In this workbook you have:

- Learned more about low mood and depression.

- Completed your own Five Areas® Assessment to identify how low mood and stress are affecting you.

- Considered possible targets for change, and decided which other workbooks you want to work on.

- Learned when you should get extra help and where to go for it.

Before you go

What have you learned from this workbook?

_____

_____

What do you want to try next?

_____

_____

Try it out

Over the next week, complete a *Five Areas® Assessment Sheet*. There is a blank one at the end of this workbook.

Choose a time when you have felt *better* and a time when you felt *worse*. Complete your five areas review as soon afterwards as possible. Try to see how each of the areas is affecting you on these occasions. Does this affect what workbooks you'd want to work on next?

Worksheets to help you practice

Practice is important to help you master this approach. You can get free access to additional worksheets used in this workbook chapter and the wider book at www.llttf.com/resources

From the current workbook, this includes an additional copy of the *Five Areas® Assessment Sheet* (Figure 2.2).

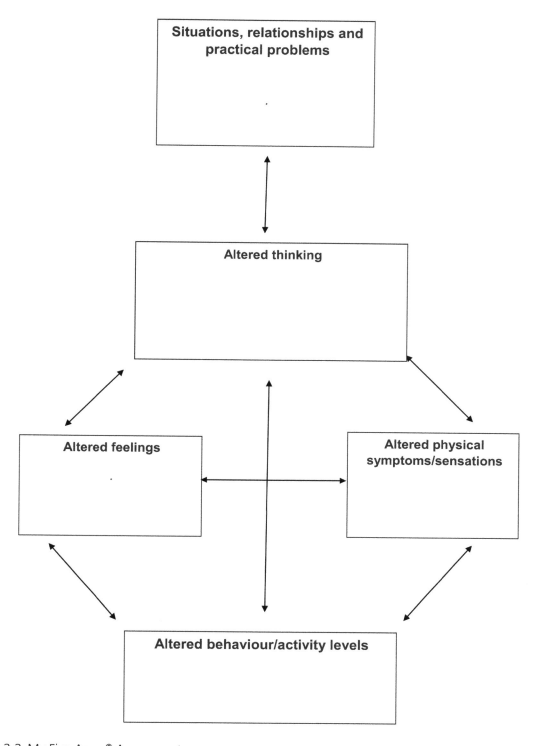

Figure 2.2 My Five Areas® Assessment

Acknowledgements

The cartoon illustrations were produced by Keith Chan, kchan75@hotmail.com. Thank you to Mrs Theresa Kelly and Mrs Sue Wood at Five Areas Ltd for their helpful advice and comments on earlier drafts of this book. Also, to those practitioners and Peer mentors at North West Senior and Disability Services in Oregon, USA who inputted into the initial modifications of these resources to suit an older adult readership.

PART 2

Tackling problems and rebalancing relationships

Overcoming Depression and Low Mood in Older Adults

A Five Areas® CBT Approach

Practical problem solving

Dr Chris Williams

DOI: 10.4324/9781003347637-5

Do you ever notice this?

Is this you?

If so, … this workbook is for you.

In this workbook you will:

• Identify practical problems in your own life.

• See an example of problem solving in practice and apply it to a problem of your own.

How practical problems affect us

Everyone faces some problems and difficulties in life. This workbook focuses on practical problems outside us. People often experience practical difficulties from time to time. Sometimes these are larger issues – like a debt or a leaking roof. Sometimes they are smaller everyday hassles that can add up, like having to do the shopping and post some letters. Often, we can cope when there's just one small problem. But when we face a particularly difficult or large problem or a whole range of smaller things happening at the same time, we can struggle to cope and may feel overwhelmed. This is especially so when we're feeling tired poorly or stressed.

It can help to think about how you are feeling in the Five Areas® of your life. The first area of the Five Areas® Assessment contains three elements: the different situations, relationships and practical problems that we face. But these problems don't just remain outside us. They can affect what we think (altered thinking – Area 2), how we feel emotionally (altered feelings – Area 3), and how we react in our bodies (altered physical symptoms/bodily sensations – Area 4), and, finally, all add up to affect what we do (our altered behaviour or activity levels – Area 5).

You can see these illustrated in Figure 3.1. See how each area affects each other. So, *situations, relationship issues and practical problems and challenges outside us:* such as bills to pay, an argument with a friend, having a leaky roof and all the mess that causes or facing an overgrown garden....

Lead to *altered thinking*: where we dwell on these worries, and can't get them out of our mind. The worries build up and up, distressing us, and we think we can't cope …

Leads to *altered feelings*: Feeling anxious, stressed, scared, angry or perhaps guilty that we aren't coping. Strong emotions then lead to *altered physical symptoms/bodily sensations*: not sleeping, feeling physically tense, which is exhausting making us feel worn down.

All of these different changes then add up to *affect our behaviour/activity levels:* If we feel overwhelmed and anxious, we might avoid the challenges we face. So, we might ignore the problem – letting it build up and up. Or give up or act as if we are overwhelmed. Or perhaps we feel angry at ourselves that we can't sort out the problem, or are angry at others because they live so far away or don't offer the help we would have expected.

Tackling these outside problems will therefore help you feel better in many of the other areas too. This workbook will help you achieve this.

Before you start

Sometimes problems occur because of things we can't control. But sometimes they're the result of things that we could have done differently.

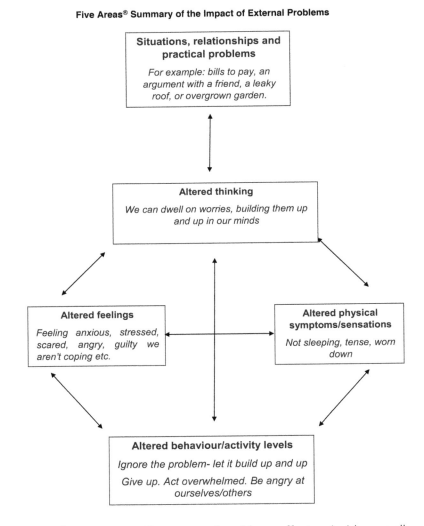

Five Areas® Summary of the Impact of External Problems

Situations, relationships and practical problems

For example: bills to pay, an argument with a friend, a leaky roof, or overgrown garden.

Altered thinking

We can dwell on worries, building them up and up in our minds

Altered feelings

Feeling anxious, stressed, scared, angry, guilty we aren't coping etc.

Altered physical symptoms/sensations

Not sleeping, tense, worn down

Altered behaviour/activity levels

Ignore the problem- let it build up and up

Give up. Act overwhelmed. Be angry at ourselves/others

Figure 3.1 Our Five Areas® Assessment: How external problems affect us inside as well

For example:

- Problems in relationships may build up because one person kept expecting the other person to do something without making it clear what was needed. So, the answer there might be to ask for what we need more clearly by *Being assertive*.

- Or, perhaps someone didn't respond in helpful ways that would have prevented things from worsening at an earlier stage (*'a stitch in time'*).

- Or, maybe a problem of debt has built up because of problem gambling or drinking? In this case the *Unhelpful things you do* workbook might be of help.

Therefore, before you start working on the plan you need to think about three things:

- *Your behaviour*: Do you find that the same kinds of problems occur again and again? If so, is there anything that you keep doing (or not doing) that leads to the problem? If you answered 'Yes', you may find the workbook on *Unhelpful things you do* useful.

- *Your thinking*: Is it possible that things are being blown up out of proportion because of how you feel inside at the moment? If you think this may be so, then try reading the *Noticing* or *Changing unhelpful thinking workbooks* to help you get things back into perspective.

- *Other people and other ways of support:* Some problems are hard to change by yourself. For example it's common for someone who is vulnerable to elder abuse to keep quiet and hide the problem. If this is you, reach out to others for support – including your doctor or the Police if needed.

It's important when facing problems to also be aware of the resources and abilities you have available to you.

Make a list of any practical resources and supports that you have:

_____

_____

At times of distress, are you only aware of just the problems? This can make you overlook the supports you listed above even though they are there. Remember, the resources you have listed may be part of your solution.

How to tackle problems

- Approach each problem separately and, in turn.

- Define the problem clearly so that you are focused on your work.

- But what if the problem seems really huge or really complicated? Well, when problems are large like that, it's a bit like facing the challenge of how would you eat an elephant.

How do you eat an elephant – or if you are vegetarian, a huge turnip? Of course, you'd eat it one bite at a time. In the same way, you can break down any problem – no matter how large or complicated, into smaller parts that are then easier to solve.

Have a clear plan

You will need to decide:

- **Short-term** targets – changes you can make today, tomorrow and next week.

- **Medium-term** targets – changes over the next few weeks.

- **Long-term** targets – where you want to be in six months or a year.

That way you can tackle even very big or complicated problems step by step.

The seven steps to problem solving

Step 1: Identify and clearly define what you are going to work on

Below is a checklist of common difficult situations, practical and relationship problems. Are any of these affecting you?

Most people face a range of smaller or larger issues every day, so it's likely that you will have noticed problems in at least some of these areas. You can also add any other problems to the space at the end of the table.

Am I facing any difficult situations, relationships or practical issues?	Yes	No	Sometimes
I have worries about money or debts.	☐	☐	☐
There are problems where I live.	☐	☐	☐
I/somebody close to me doesn't have a job.	☐	☐	☐
I'm finding it difficult doing everything around the house/garden.	☐	☐	☐
I don't have time to meet my commitments outside the house/family.	☐	☐	☐
There's something I can't afford to buy or borrow.	☐	☐	☐
There's much too much to do.	☐	☐	☐
There's something practical I don't understand that I need to find out about.	☐	☐	☐
There's an item that's broken/damaged/leaking that needs fixing.	☐	☐	☐
Relationship issues	**Yes**	**No**	**Sometimes**
There is no one around who I can talk to and I'm lonely.	☐	☐	☐
I have relationship issues (such as arguments) with my partner/spouse/adult children.	☐	☐	☐
My partner/spouse doesn't really talk to me or offer me enough support.	☐	☐	☐
I'm not spending enough time with my children/grandchildren.	☐	☐	☐
Family/carer staff won't do what I ask them.	☐	☐	☐
Someone close to me has alcohol or drug problems.	☐	☐	☐
Someone close to me has problems with the police or courts.	☐	☐	☐
Someone close to me is being threatened by somebody.	☐	☐	☐
Someone close to me is being unkind/threatening to me/someone else.	☐	☐	☐
There's someone else, like a sick relative, I have to care for.	☐	☐	☐
I have difficulties with others, for example neighbours/other residents/friends.	☐	☐	☐

Write down any other difficult situations, relationships or practical issues you are facing here (remember, these are problems outside you).

_____

_____

 EXAMPLE: Susan's problem

Susan is no longer fit enough to keep up with her garden. She is upset because her garden has become overgrown. Her family has promised to help out – but haven't got round to coming over. She sits at the window feeling upset that the garden has got into this state.

Susan completes the checklist and selects the following item from the list as her problem area:

I'm finding it difficult doing everything around the house/garden.

Now it's your turn

Complete the checklist. Look back at your responses and choose one problem that you will tackle first. This is particularly important if you have checked many boxes in the list. It isn't possible to overcome all these problems at once, so you need to decide which **one** area to focus on.

My target problem: Write down the one problem area you want to work on first.

Remember that this should be a situation, practical or relationship problem.

_____

_____

Break complicated problems down into smaller steps

The important thing is to use a **step-by-step** approach where no single step seems too large. The first step needs to be something that gets you moving in the right direction. For many larger or more complicated problems, there may be lots going on.

 EXAMPLE: Susan's step-by-step approach

It would make a huge difference if the front and back lawns could be cut. This would make a big difference to the whole appearance and is a good first step.

You may need to break down your target into many smaller steps that you can tackle one at a time.

Now decide whether you need to **break your own target into smaller steps**.

Q Is it a big and difficult task? Do you need to break it down into smaller, more achievable steps that you can tackle over the next week or two?

Yes ☐   No ☐

Break your own problem into smaller steps if you need to. If so, write down your revised first target here:

_____

_____

Step 2: Think up as many solutions as possible to achieve your first target

When you feel overwhelmed by practical problems, it can seem hard to even start tackling them.

One way around this is to step back from the problem(s) and see if any other solutions are possible. Be creative. The more solutions that you can think of, the more likely it is that a good one will emerge.

KEY POINT

Try to include ridiculous ideas at first as you are trying to come up with as many ideas as possible to make it easier for you to identify a good solution. Thinking up unusual or ridiculous solutions first may help you get your creative ideas flowing.

Some people find they can come up with more solutions when they ask themselves:

Q What advice would you give a friend who was trying to solve a similar problem?

(Sometimes it's easier to think of solutions for others than for ourselves).

_____

_____

Also:

Q What helpful ideas would others suggest? (e.g. family, friends or other people you know such as clergy).

_____

_____

What have you tried in the past that was helpful?

_____

_____

 EXAMPLE: Susan's problem – possible solutions

Susan's list includes creative ideas that include some unusual or ridiculous suggestions in order to help her be as creative as possible in her possible solutions.

Just ignore the overgrowth.

Use my savings to get a gardening team in to cut the grass.

Ask my family to help again.

Look at whether I'm entitled to any grants or benefits?

I could ask for help from the local Church or other places of worship.

Set fire to the grass at the end of summer.

Get a robot lawnmower.

Put a "Help Wanted" sign up at the local shop.

Now write down as many possible solutions (including unusual or ridiculous ideas) for your own problem:

_____

_____

_____

_____

_____

_____

_____

_____

Step 3: Look at the pros and cons of each possible solution

Just ignore the overgrowth.

Pros: Easier in the short term.

Cons: My eyes keep being drawn to it. It's very upsetting. I'm letting the neighbours and street down.

Use my savings to get a gardening team in to do cut the grass.

   Pros: The job would be done quickly. They would take the cuttings away.

   Cons: I don't know anyone who could do it. I don't have many savings.

Ask my family to help again.

   Pros: No or low cost.

   Cons: They haven't helped before. They might not have time or interest.

Look at whether I'm entitled to any grants or benefits.

   Pros: I've friends who get grants like Attendance Allowance. It's quite a lot of money and that could pay towards a gardener.

   Cons: I might not qualify. There would be a delay.

I could ask for help from my local church or other places of worship.

   Pros: I've been for so many years. I know lots of people.

   Cons: People are so busy these days. Maybe they have forgotten me.

Set fire to the grass at the end of summer.

   Pros: It might clear it.

   Cons: It's not realistic. The fire might spread. The neighbours would complain about the smoke. It sounds very dangerous.

Get a robot lawn mower.

   Pros: I saw them in the newspaper. They sound good.

   Cons: They are way too expensive – hundreds of pounds! Also, you have to fit control wires round the garden, and it couldn't go up my garden steps. I can't be doing with that.

Put a help wanted sign up in the local shop.

   Pros: It might work.

   Cons: I'd rather get a proper gardener. I'm not sure I'd trust them. Would they take my money and not do the work?

Write your own list of ideas below and the pros and cons of each suggestion.

My own suggestions from Step 2	Pros/Advantages	Cons/Disadvantages

Step 4: Now choose one of the solutions

In making your decision, keep in mind that the best way of tackling a problem is to plan **slow, steady changes.**

KEY POINT

The solution you are looking for is something that gets you moving in the right direction. This should be small enough to be possible, but big enough to move you forward.

EXAMPLE: **Susan's final choice**

Susan tries to choose an option that will be realistic and likely to succeed. She makes her decision after looking at all the pros and cons she's listed in Step 3.

Susan decides on balance to first ask her friends at church. Many of the other suggestions might also work, but this suggestion seems like a reasonable first step.

Look at your own responses in Step 3 and then choose a solution.

My solution

Write down your preferred option here:

_____

_____

Step 5: Plan the steps needed to carry out your chosen solution

You need to have a clear plan that lays out exactly **what** you are going to do and **when** you are going to do it. Write down the steps needed to carry out your plan.

This will help you to think about what to do and also to predict possible problems that might arise. Remember, that an important part of the planning process is to predict what would block the plan. That way you can think about how you will respond if there are problems to keep your plan on track.

EXAMPLE: **Susan's plan.**

List who I know, using the names and contact information I have to hand. I know the clergy office number and can phone them. I'll do that today after lunch at 2 pm as someone is often in then.

Now, write down your plan.

Q **What** are you going to do?

_____

_____

_____

Q **When** are you going to do it (day and time)?

_____

_____

Q **What** problems or difficulties could arise? How could you overcome them?

_____

_____

Check your plan:

Now see if you can answer 'Yes' to the questions below.

Q Useful for understanding or changing how I am?

Yes ☐   No ☐

Q Clear and specific, so that I will know when I have done it?

Yes ☐   No ☐

Q Realistic, practical and achievable?

Yes ☐   No ☐

Q What problems or difficulties could arise?

_____

_____

 EXAMPLE: Susan's backup solution if there is a problem

If there is no one in the Church Office, I'll leave a message on the answerphone. If they say no, I'll pay a local gardner as a short-term fix, and also take the slow route and ask social services about applying for Attendance allowance.

Step 6: Carry out your plan

Now carry out your plan at the time you planned it. Good luck!

Step 7: Review the outcome

Whatever happens, now is the time to review what happened.

Afterwards, even if it went well, stop and reflect on how things went. If things didn't go as you wanted, again try to *stop, think and reflect* so you can learn from this. That way you can put what you're learning into practice so you make better and better plans going forward.

EXAMPLE **1**: Susan's plan works well.

The Minister answers the phone and agrees to arrange help. Three days later someone from the church congregation committee gets in touch saying there are two volunteers who will come. They will bring their own equipment. They attend and cut both lawns, removing the cuttings. They say they can help do the same regularly.

What went well? *It was a good solution*.

What didn't go so well? *Nothing really*.

What have you learned about from what happened? *It's okay to ask for help*.

EXAMPLE **2**: Susan's plan doesn't work well.

Susan calls the church and they are too busy to help because of illness. Susan thanks them. She decides to pay someone in the short term to cut just the front lawn. She also contacts Citizen's Advice for a benefits review, and is advised she is eligible for Attendance Allowance. She gets this – and this allows her to engage a regular gardener.

If you noticed problems with your plan

Choosing realistic targets for change is important. Think back to where you started. Were you too ambitious or unrealistic in choosing the target you did? Sometimes your attempt to solve a problem may be blocked by something unexpected. Perhaps something didn't happen as you planned or someone reacted in an unexpected way? Try to learn from what happened.

How could you change how you approach the problem based on any problems that arise?

_____

_____

Planning the next steps

Did your plan help you to tackle the problem you were working on completely? If not, you may need to plan out other solutions to tackle what is left of your problem.

For example in Susan's situation, where she still has overgrown hedges and shrubbery and borders that need work.

What about you? What is the next bit of the problem you want to work on?

The important thing is to build one step upon another.

So, you now have the choice to:

- Focus on the same problem area and plan to keep working on it one step at a time.

- Or choose a new problem area to work on.

Consider your **short-term, medium-term and longer-term** targets. This means, where you want to be in a few weeks' time (short term), in a few months' time (medium term) or in a year's time (long term).

 EXAMPLE: Susan's next steps

Susan uses her Attendance allowance to get a gardening company to come and do a one-off clearance to cut everything back. She can now afford to have them come and keep on top of the shrubs and hedges twice a year.

Now it's your turn.

Your own next steps

When making your next plan:

It's helpful to:

- Plan to work on **only** one or two key problems over the next week.

- Plan to alter things slowly in a step-by-step way.

- Use blank Seven Steps of Problem solving sheet (copies available at www.llttf.com/resources) to check that each step is always well planned. That way you know exactly what you are going to do and when you'll do it.

It's unhelpful to:

- Try to start to alter too many things all at once.

- Choose something that is too hard a target to start with.

- Talk yourself out of trying to sort out the problem by saying '*It won't work*' or '*It's a waste of time*'. Instead, try the plan out and see what happens. You may be pleasantly surprised.

Write your own short-, medium- and long-term plans here:

Short term – What might you do over the next week or so? This is your next step that you need to plan.

_____

_____

_____

Medium term – What might you aim towards doing over the next few weeks and the next few steps?

_____

_____

_____

Longer term – Where do you want to be in a few months or so?

_____

_____

_____

Remember to plan slow, steady changes. By breaking down problems and tackling them one step at a time any problem can be addressed.

When you need more help

Remember, you are not alone. If you need more help, consider asking:

- People around you, whom you know and trust.
- Your doctor or other health or social care worker.
- Your local Citizens Advice Office.
- Specialist services and voluntary organisations for help with problems such as debt, housing difficulty and relationship counselling. They can be part of your plan.

SUMMARY

In this workbook you have:

- Learned how to identify problems in your own life.
- Seen an example of problem solving in practice and had a chance to apply this to one of your own problems.

Before you go

What have you learned from this workbook?

_____

_____

What do you want to try next?

_____

_____

Over the next week, complete a blank *Seven steps to problem solving* worksheet to work on a larger or smaller problem.

Notice any change solving or improving a problem has on your mood, thinking, activity and body.

Worksheets to help you practice

Practice is important to help you master this approach. You can get free access to additional worksheets used in this workbook chapter and the wider book at www.llttf.com/resources

From the current workbook, this includes an additional copy of the *Seven Steps to Problem solving worksheets.*

Acknowledgements

The cartoon illustrations were produced by Keith Chan, kchan75@hotmail.com. Thank you to Mrs Theresa Kelly and Mrs Sue Wood at Five Areas Ltd for their helpful advice and comments on earlier drafts of this book. Also, to those practitioners and Peer mentors at North West Senior and Disability Services in Oregon, USA who inputted into the initial modifications of these resources to suit an older adult readership.

The term Five Areas® is a registered trademark of Five Areas Resources Ltd. Although we hope you find this book helpful, it's not intended to be a direct substitute for consultative advice with a healthcare professional, nor do we give any assurance about its effectiveness in a particular case. Accordingly, neither we nor the author shall be held liable for any loss or damages arising from its use.

Overcoming Depression and Low Mood in Older Adults

A Five Areas® CBT Approach

Being assertive

Dr Chris Williams

DOI: 10.4324/9781003347637-6

Do you ever notice this?

I really resent having to do EVERYTHING at home because my spouse can't help

I can't say no to my children and grandchildren

My friends expect me to drive them everywhere

If the warden says that one more time, I'll give them a piece of my mind!

People won't like me if I don't volunteer at church

People know not to push me around

My partner expects me to do the gardening just like it used to be- and it's too much for me now

I wish I could just ask for what I really want

I can't stand up for myself

Is this you?

If so, … this workbook is for you.

In this workbook you will:

- Learn about the differences between passive behaviour, aggressive behaviour and assertive behaviour.

- Learn the rules of assertion and how you can put them into practice in everyday situations.

What is assertiveness?

 KEY POINT

Assertiveness is about being able to make sure your opinions and feelings are considered. You can be assertive without being forceful or rude.

Assertiveness means:

- Letting others know about your feelings, needs, rights and opinions while maintaining respect for other people.

- Expressing your feelings in a direct, honest and appropriate way.

- Realising it's possible to stand up for your rights in such a way that you don't disregard another person's rights at the same time.

Assertion is not **about winning**, but about being able to walk away feeling that you put across what you wanted to say.

Try to think about a time when someone else has been assertive with you and respected your opinion.

 How did you feel about them and yourself?

About me – I felt:

_____

_____

_____

About them – I felt:

_____

_____

_____

Benefits of being assertive

Assertiveness is an **attitude** toward yourself and others that is helpful, straightforward and honest. When you are being assertive, you ask for what you want:

- Directly and openly.

- Appropriately, respecting everyone's opinions and rights.

- Confidently, without undue anxiety.

By being assertive, you try **not** to:

- Disregard other people's rights.

- Expect other people to magically know what you want.

- Freeze with anxiety and avoid expressing yourself.

Being assertive improves your self-confidence and others' respect for you.

What do you do in difficult situations?

However confident you are, there are times when almost everyone finds it hard to deal with certain situations.

For example:

- Dealing with unhelpful shop staff.

- Asking to have '*you*' time for yourself.

- Times when your family wants to do everything for you, taking your independence away.

- Asking someone to return something they have borrowed.

- Letting your family or friends know how you feel and what you need.

- Saying no to other people's demands/requests.

Do you sometimes deal with these situations by **losing your temper**, by **saying nothing** or by **giving in?** If you do, have you noticed that it can leave you feeling unhappy, angry or feeling out of control?

How can you become more assertive?

While growing up, people learn to relate to others from their parents, teachers and friends. You may also be influenced by other things in wider society such as TV and magazines. You may have come to believe how important it is to be a 'perfect' parent and grandparent and do a great job of this all the time. But in trying to do this, you can become so focused on doing things for other people that you may forget to do things for yourself as well.

Sometimes your confidence can get worn away. For example if someone has been bullied or ridiculed when they were growing up, or is criticised a lot by their family, that someone could

Being assertive   **53**

lose their confidence. In these situations, you may learn to **react passively or aggressively** to people and situations.

> **KEY POINT**
>
> The good news is that although you may have learned to react passively or aggressively in life, you can become more assertive by learning *assertiveness skills*.

Key elements of passive behaviour

Behaving passively means:

- Always saying *'Yes'* and giving in to the demands of others.

- Not letting others know about your feelings, needs, rights and opinions; and

- Always choosing others' needs over your own.

Usually, people behave passively to **avoid conflict** and to **please others**. This kind of behaviour is driven by a fear of not wanting to upset others, or a fear that others won't like us. But, in the longer term, this can make you feel worse and less and less confident.

When you behave passively, others begin to expect this of you and may take you for granted and increasingly expect you to drop everything to help them.

Key elements of aggressive behaviour

Aggression is the opposite of assertion. Behaving aggressively means:

- Demanding things in an angry or threatening way, and not respecting other people.

- Thinking your own needs are more important than those of others. An aggressive person ignores other people's needs and thinks they have little or nothing to contribute.

The aim of aggression is to win, even at the expense of others.

Overall, in the long term, being aggressive causes additional problems for the person and for the people around them. An additional issue as we get older is that sometimes this can affect how well we filter what we say. When we are younger we are more able to recognise when we should hold back and think but not say something. Perhaps inappropriate jokes or comments about someone's appearance, family, background or choices. This can happen more and more as a part of ageing but also might be a symptom that occurs after illnesses such as transient ischaemic attacks or a stroke.

> **KEY POINT**
>
> Behaving aggressively or being passive can be changed by learning the skill of 'assertive communication'.

Overcoming Depression and Low Mood in Older Adults: A Five Areas® CBT Approach   © 2024 Five Areas Resources Limited

So, assertiveness means stating clearly what you expect and making sure that what you want is considered as well as what other people want or need.

You can learn and practice being assertive. By practicing being assertive, you'll become more aware of your own needs as an individual.

The rules of assertion

The following 12 rules can help you live your life more assertively.

I have the right to:

- Respect myself – who I am and what I do.

- Recognise my own needs as an individual, that is separate from what's expected of me in particular roles, such as 'grandparent', 'mother', 'brother', 'partner', 'daughter', 'son' or 'wife'.

- Make clear 'I' statements about how I feel and what I think, for example *'I feel very uncomfortable with your decision'*.

- Recognise that it's normal to make mistakes.

- Change my mind, if I choose.

- Ask for 'thinking about it time'. For example when people ask you to do something, you have the right to say *'I would like to think it over and I will let you know by the end of the week'*.

- Allow myself to enjoy my successes, that is being pleased with what I've done and sharing it with others.

- Ask for what I want, rather than hoping someone will notice what I want.

- Recognise that I am not responsible for the behaviour of other adults or for pleasing other adults all the time.

- Respect other people and their right to be assertive and expect the same respect in return.

- Say, 'I don't understand'. So, you make sure you work out what is happening.

- Deal with others without depending on them for approval.

The 12 Rules of Assertion

I can:	Do you believe this rule is true?		Have you applied this in the last week?	
1. Respect myself.	Yes ☐	No ☐	Yes ☐	No ☐
2. Recognise my own needs as an individual independent of others.	Yes ☐	No ☐	Yes ☐	No ☐
3. Make clear 'I' statements about how I feel and what I think, for example 'I feel very uncomfortable with your decision'.	Yes ☐	No ☐	Yes ☐	No ☐
4. Allow myself to make mistakes.	Yes ☐	No ☐	Yes ☐	No ☐

5. Change my mind.	Yes ☐	No ☐	Yes ☐	No ☐
6. Ask for 'thinking about it' time.	Yes ☐	No ☐	Yes ☐	No ☐
7. Allow myself to enjoy my successes.	Yes ☐	No ☐	Yes ☐	No ☐
8. Ask for what I want, rather than hoping someone will notice what I want.	Yes ☐	No ☐	Yes ☐	No ☐
9. Recognise that I am not responsible for the behaviour of others or for pleasing others all the time.	Yes ☐	No ☐	Yes ☐	No ☐
10. Respect other people and their right to be assertive and expect the same in return.	Yes ☐	No ☐	Yes ☐	No ☐
11. Say, 'I don't understand'.	Yes ☐	No ☐	Yes ☐	No ☐
12. Deal with others without being dependent on them for approval or need to please.	Yes ☐	No ☐	Yes ☐	No ☐

You can put your rights into practice to develop assertiveness skills by using several assertiveness techniques. Some of these are described below. Before learning assertiveness techniques, it's sometimes also important to consider how to start a conversation.

Starting and maintaining conversations

Sometimes you can feel isolated if there is no one around to talk to. Perhaps you may feel lonely, and lack contact with anyone. There are many practical things you can do to begin to meet people.

For example:

- Making friends through people you know already.

- Joining an exercise class, community choir, walking club or some other group class at your local or community centre or a book club or crafting class.

- Taking a course, such as an adult evening class to learn a new language. Or joining a club, for example at your local community centre.

- Visiting other local places where you can meet others, for example community organisations or the local place of worship. Some local shops such as hairdressers also provide a place to meet people and connect.

- Getting in touch with people you knew but haven't seen for a while. Use email, write a letter, social media or telephone to get in touch. Arrange to meet if you can.

A key step in all of these ideas is that initial 'hello'. Things often flow easier once you have overcome that initial hurdle.

If you are a bit out of practice, then here are some good conversation starters:

- How are you?

- Nice day isn't it?

- Hi, I'm new here and a little bit nervous.

KEY POINT

Remember – it doesn't matter if you talk about superficial things to begin with such as the weather, the local news or about a book you enjoyed.

You don't have to do this if you don't like it. Instead, you can think of some other conversation starters in advance. Good opening questions often begin with the words:

- **What?** – What was the meeting like last week? What did you do yesterday? What was the new movie like?

- **How?** – How did you find the meal? How are you? How are you getting on with your gardening?

- **When?** – When will we be covering this on the course? When do you start back with your volunteering?

- **Who?** – Who came yesterday? Who's that over there?

- **Why?** – Why does that happen (or not happen)? Why do we do things this way?

Follow these with **back-up questions** to keep the conversation going. For example:

- Who came yesterday – did they enjoy it?

- What did they say?

- Did it go well?

- Do you think they'll come back?

- And, of course, remember to listen!

KEY POINT

Conversation is a skill you can develop with practice. Follow these suggestions and slowly you'll start to relax and enjoy your time with others.

Assertiveness skills: Saying 'no'

Many people find that 'no' can seem to be one of the hardest words to say. Try to remember when you may have found yourself in situations that you didn't want to be in, just because you had avoided saying this one simple word.

Why does this happen? People often worry that they may be seen as being mean and selfish, or they may worry about confrontation or being rejected by others. This may prevent you using the word NO when you need it.

 Do I have a problem saying 'No'?

Yes ☐   No ☐   Sometimes ☐

If you checked '*Yes*' or '*Sometimes*', try to practice saying '*No*' by using the following techniques:

- Be straightforward and honest so that you can make your point effectively.

- This isn't the same as being rude.

- Tell the person if you are finding it hard to say 'No', but on this occasion, you must.

- Don't apologise and give all sorts of reasons for saying 'No'. It is okay to say 'No' if you don't want to do something.

- Remember that it is better in the long run to be truthful than breed resentment and bitterness within yourself.

'*Broken record*'

This refers to the situation where the needle gets stuck in a groove of a record – and plays and then replays the same lines again and again. In the broken record assertiveness technique, you do the same when it comes to asking for what you need, or saying 'No'.

First, practice what you want to say by **repeating over and over again** what you want or need. During the conversation, keep returning to your prepared lines, stating clearly what it is you need or want. Don't be put off by clever arguments or by what the other person says. Once you have prepared the lines you want to say, you can relax. This works in virtually any situation. Often it turns out better than you expected.

 EXAMPLE: Being firm about what you want

Jane: 'Can I borrow £20 from you?'

Paul: 'I cannot lend you any money. I've run out'.

Jane 'I'll pay you back as soon as I can. I need it desperately.

You are my friend aren't you?'

Paul: 'I cannot lend you any money'.

Jane: 'I would do the same for you. You won't miss £20'.

Paul: 'I am your friend but I cannot lend you any money. I'm afraid I can't afford it just now'.

Remember:

- Work out beforehand what you want to say.

- Repeat your reply over and over again and stick to what you have decided to say.

Body language and assertiveness

How people communicate involves more than just words. Your voice tone, how quickly and loudly you speak, eye contact and body posture – all affect how you come across to others.

When you're being assertive be aware of the non-verbal communication you transmit as well as the words you say.

Eye contact

- Meet the other person's eyes from time to time.

- Make eye contact – but don't end up staring at the person.

- Try not to look down or away for too long – this may seem rude and off-putting to others.

If you find this hard to do, practice looking just past the person. For example look at a thing such as a picture on the wall behind them. Or look at their forehead or nose. This allows you to show you are paying attention – but without directly meeting the other person's eyes.

Your voice

- Try to vary your tone so you come over as interested and interesting.

- Don't be afraid of silence – especially if you've asked a question. When you ask a question, you may be tempted to fill any uncomfortable gaps yourself. Be prepared to allow a little silence. Likewise, you don't need to reply instantly to any question. Remember that you're allowed some time to think.

If someone is anxious about speaking, then it's common for them to speak more quickly and loudly. Consider how quickly or loudly you talk. Aim for a relaxed yet serious manner if you can.

Posture

- Think about how you hold your body:

- Try looking up and don't hunch over – this can happen when you feel vulnerable or anxious.

- Keep an appropriate distance ('personal space') between you and the other person.

- Don't get too close – this might be seen as aggressive or inappropriate (unless you know the person very well).

Be friendly

Smiling and laughing once in a while is a friendly thing to do. People will often smile back. It has to be natural, though, and not forced (remember those politicians on TV).

Be relaxed in your body

- Think about how you hold your body. If you're tense or anxious you may clench your fists and frown which may come over as being aggressive.

- Relax your body. Quickly think about how you are holding your arms and shoulders and try to relax tense muscles. Some people tend to pull up their shoulders towards their ears when they feel tense. Drop them down and relax. You'll feel better for it.

A word of caution

Don't think you have to suddenly get all of this right immediately. You should make these changes slowly – over many weeks or even months.

You shouldn't get too concerned about whether you are avoiding eye contact or smiling enough. All you need to do is be aware of this and try to occasionally make some small changes in what you do. Experiment and see what works for you.

Trying out being more assertive

Think about the following when you plan to respond assertively. Choose:

- **The right person.** Some people can take even assertive feedback badly. If you know that what you say is likely to be misinterpreted, or that the person will over-react, then you need to get some extra help such as from a close friend or a family member.

- **The right time.** For example try not to start talking about important things as soon as your partner, family member, or carer arrives, or if you notice they are not in an approachable mood. Maybe they are worried about something in their own lives or feel tired. Choose a more relaxed time – or plan such a time – for example plan to go for a walk together.

- **The right issue.** The issue needs to be something that the other person can change. For example asking your son or daughter to take care of all your business and personal care needs is most likely not to be realistic. Instead, you may ask them to help you seek some alternatives.

- **The right words.** Use the approaches described in this workbook ('*Broken record*' and '*Saying no*'). These techniques will help you to say what you need.

SUMMARY

In this workbook you have learned:

- The differences between passive behaviour, aggressive behaviour and assertive behaviour.

- About the rules of assertion and how you can put them into practice in everyday life.

Before you go

What have you learned from this workbook?

_____

_____

What do you want to try next?

_____

_____

Think about how you can be more assertive in your own life. If you recognise that you lack assertiveness, try to:

- Use one of the two assertiveness techniques (broken record and saying no) during the next week.

- Remind yourself about and put into practice the **12 rules of assertion**. Copy or use your phone to photograph the list and carry them around with you. Put it somewhere you will see it (for example by your TV or on a door, mirror or on the fridge) to remind you of these rules.

View this as an action plan that can help you to change how you are and also to learn something new about yourself and other people.

Worksheets to help you practice

Practice is important to help you master this approach. You can get free access to additional worksheets used in this workbook chapter and the wider book at www.llttf.com/resources

Acknowledgements

The cartoon illustrations were produced by Keith Chan, kchan75@hotmail.com. Thank you to Mrs Theresa Kelly and Mrs Sue Wood at Five Areas Ltd for their helpful advice and comments on earlier drafts of this book. Also, to those practitioners and Peer mentors at North West Senior and Disability Services in Oregon, USA who inputted into the initial modifications of these resources to suit an older adult readership.

The term Five Areas® is a registered trademark of Five Areas Resources Ltd. Although we hope you find this book helpful, it's not intended to be a direct substitute for consultative advice with a healthcare professional, nor do we give any assurance about its effectiveness in a particular case. Accordingly, neither we nor the author shall be held liable for any loss or damages arising from its use.

Overcoming Depression and Low Mood in Older Adults

A Five Areas® CBT Approach

Building relationships with your family and friends

Dr Chris Williams

DOI: 10.4324/9781003347637-7

Do you ever notice this?

Is this you?

If so, … this workbook is for you.

In this workbook you will:

- Review your own style of communicating with others.

- Learn how to build (and rebuild) close relationships with the people around you.

- Discover a three-step approach to controlling anger.

The Five Areas® and your relationships

Low mood can affect you in each of five key areas of your life. As well as the people and events around us, these include your thinking, feelings, physical symptoms/sensations and behaviour/activities. All these can alter the relationships around us are causing problems. We can often feel low or anxious because of changes in our relationships. Also, if we feel low or stressed, it can affect how we relate to others.

Relating to other adults

Some people have many friends and acquaintances. Others prefer to keep to themselves and are 'close' to fewer people. You may also find that over the years you start to lose people you've been close to over the years. Old school friends, workmates, neighbours and others. This may leave you feeling lonely, or reduce your opportunities to get out and about meeting people locally or further afield.

Perhaps other changes have occurred because of events like retirement. This may provide new opportunities such as moving house. But house moves also can take us away from familiar people and places near where we used to live.

You may also find that retirement brings other challenges. More time on your hands and no work commitments might have sounded lovely, but sometimes we can miss the benefits of work. Something to get up for each day, meeting people as a result of work, the benefits of a job well done, job satisfaction and being needed – and of course the additional income that is lost. These are discussed more in the workbook *Doing things that make you feel better*.

If you have a partner or spouse, retirement might allow you more time to spend together. That might be lots of fun, allowing you to travel or do other things you've always dreamed of doing. However, sometimes spending more time together may bring out minor (or major) resentments that have perhaps simmered over the years, but have been coped with because one or both partners have been out at work or socialising. Spending more time together offers more chances that these sorts of disagreements can come out.

How do you relate to others you are close to?

The following questions will help you recognise your own attitudes and reactions towards the people you are close to. It may be tempting to answer these questions quickly with what you think as the 'correct' answer. Instead, use the questions as an opportunity to reflect on the answers. The purpose of this task is to help you to recognise the things that may need to change for you to build more balanced relationships.

How do I respond to people I am close to – and how do they respond to me? Think back on your current and past close relationships including friendships.

Q What *helpful* relationship styles do you repeat? (Things you do that build closeness and respect.)

_____

_____

Q What *unhelpful* relationship styles do you repeat? (Things you do that damage closeness and reduce respect.)

_____

_____

Q How do these patterns affect your relationships – now and in the past?

_____

_____

Q How might these factors affect how you respond when you feel distressed or are struggling?

_____

_____

Q Do you often feel uncomfortable when speaking about how you or someone close to you feels?

_____

_____

Q Do you try to avoid speaking about how you feel? How do those around you react to this?

_____

_____

Q How have your relationships changed as you age or since the onset of any disability/long-term illness?

_____

_____

Things you can do that can make a difference

The following are some responses that can help build your relationships and friendships.

With people you don't know so well (like neighbours or people you meet)

It's helpful to:

- Be yourself.

- Have planned a one-line statement of how you are if someone asks *'How are you?'* Remember, they don't know you well. They may well not be aware you are finding things difficult at the moment. Don't feel you have to tell the person everything about yourself. Say something like *'Getting on well thanks. How are you?'*, and leave it at that.

It's usually not helpful to:

- Tell everyone about every aspect of your life and how you feel.

With trusted friends and family members

Your wider family and friends can be a great support for you. A separate workbook *Information for families and friends – how can you offer the best support?* – has been written for them. You might wish to show that workbook to them or even go through it together.

It's helpful to:

- Seek out support from close friends.

It's not helpful to:

- Push people away and try to cope by yourself when you need help.

- Become overly focused on just one relationship, for example just one friend

With your partner/spouse

Your partner/spouse or your boyfriend/girlfriend may be your closest support and companion. So, this relationship can have a big effect on how you feel. Sometimes difficulties may arise and there may be anger, jealousy, boredom or even affairs. These problems often are the result of a breakdown of communication and even love.

- **Communication.** Communication problems can happen in any relationship, but it becomes more difficult when you are low or stressed. You may not feel like talking for long, or welcome physical intimacy or hugs. Sometimes these changes are sudden, but more often they build up slowly over the months and years. After a while, you may find you have nothing to say. You may find it hard to even start a conversation. Your partner feels like a stranger.

- **Sex.** You may lose interest in sex or become anxious about whether you are still as attractive.

- **The Internet.** You may develop a sense of emotional closeness with someone by chatting with them online. But be careful that this doesn't replace the closeness and support that people around you can offer. Be aware that some online options may damage your real relationships by stopping you from committing emotionally or by taking up your time. Also, be aware that scammers can try and con adults of all ages out of their savings. They tend to pry on people who are lonely or isolated, and '*pretend*' they are in a relationship - and then suddenly need money transferring because of a fake '*crisis*' such as illness or pretending they have been stranded somewhere.

- **Affairs.** Sometimes people try to jolt themselves out of a low mood by having a one-night stand or starting an affair. Sometimes this is caused by loneliness, low self-esteem or anger or, a desire to prove attractiveness.

- **Time apart.** A symptom of a relationship in trouble is often that people make choices not to be around each other as much. Do you make excuses to be elsewhere? Do you or your partner choose to work late or go out separately more than is needed? Sometimes people cope by throwing themselves into looking after their grandchildren. Adult children or grandchildren may provide some people with the sense of emotional connection that is missing in their marriage/partner. People can drift apart even when they are in the same room, for example never really talking while watching TV.

Ultimately these problems come down to the issues of **communication** and **commitment**. Even when feelings seem to have been lost for each other, often relationships can improve again given time, communication, forgiveness and commitment.

Rebuilding relationships with a partner/spouse by building communication and commitment

A key question is how much improvement you both feel you need to make to improve things. To rebuild (or build) a relationship can sometimes come down to one partner making all the changes. But that misses the point of the need for *both* partners to discuss and work on their relationship problems together – if they both want to.

It may be that only some small changes of direction are needed. If so, some immediate things you can do together include:

- Listen – pay attention – don't just switch off and think you know what is being said. Talk about each other's day. Ask questions about the small but important details in life.

- Do things together – for example spend time eating meals together rather than separately.

- Tackle '*relationship killers*' such as often doing things apart or constantly criticising each other directly or via friends.

- Anger and guilt can eat away at a relationship – you may need to forgive your partner – or ask for **forgiveness** from them if you have done things that have caused hurt.

- Consider a regular date night just like when you first met.

- Develop physical intimacy in your everyday life at a level that you both feel happy with. Hugs, kisses and holding hands can build bridges. If you don't feel like having sex, try to discuss this. It may be difficult if one partner has a higher sex drive than the other. Try to agree that although you may not want to have sex as often (or even at all at the moment), you still might like hugs/kisses. Remember that even though you aren't interested in sex at the moment, your partner may still have their sexual needs.

- As you get older, changes in your body or illness may mean that sexual arousal may be affected by illness or side effects of medication. If so, discuss this with your doctor as well as your partner. It may be treatments for erectile dysfunction, and using lubricants can help overcome bodily changes that make sex harder. Some conditions can make arousal more difficult, so consider exploring the use of toys and see if these help as a couple or alone. Find activities that will satisfy both you and your partner's sexual needs.

- Bring back the romance – give surprises like a small gift like flowers, and compliments or cook a nice meal. It's the thought and preparation time that matters here – not the cost. Extravagant gifts are no replacement for time together.

Hearing what we expect to hear

At the heart of many relationship problems is a lack of communication. When people have drifted apart, there is likely to be blame and hurt on both sides. When someone is distressed, they can interpret things in quite extreme and unhelpful ways. This can strongly affect how two people interpret the same conversation.

People often think they know each other so well that **they think they already know what is going to be said**. So, they don't actually listen to what is being said. The trouble is that sometimes they can be wrong.

 EXAMPLE: Are you hearing what you expect to hear or are you listening to what is being said?

One partner may say something like '*That was a nice meal*': and mean this as a compliment. However, because of suspicion and upset, their partner may hear it as '*Well you've cooked something nice for once – usually you don't make much effort*'.

Experiment: Try this test to see if you both interpret the same event in the same way. Think about a time when you have both felt hurt, angry or upset. Then do this exercise when the heat has gone out of the situation. Complete the worksheets for you (Figure 5.1) and your partner (Figure 5.2) separately.

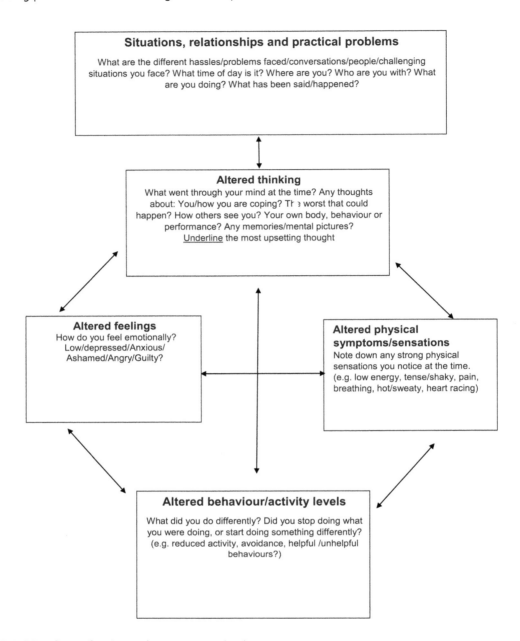

Figure 5.1 **My view** of a time when we were both upset

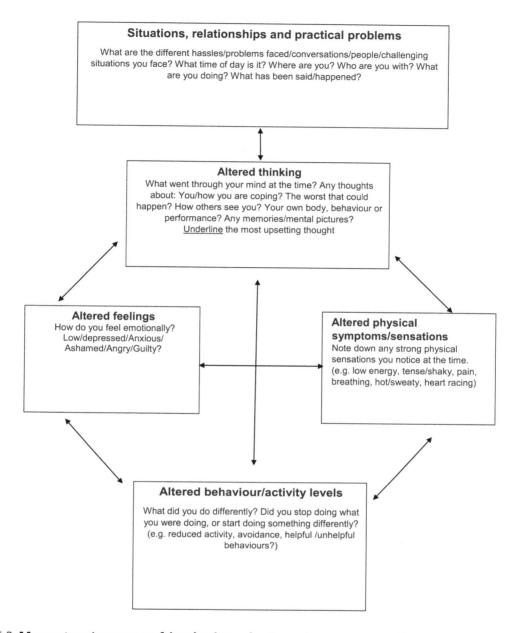

Figure 5.2 **My partner/spouse or friends view** of a time when we were both upset

Now, compare what you have both written by answering the following

Q   **How did the same situation affect how you both felt and what you did?**

_____

_____

Q   **Do you both agree on exactly what happened?**

_____

_____

Q   **Is there a difference in how you both see things?**

_____

_____

Q   **Can this help explain your different reactions to this and other upsets?**

_____

_____

Q   **Could this sort of different perception be happening again and again?**

_____

_____

You can use the same approach to help consider your conversations with other family and friends where relationship issues are becoming a problem.

Now, reflect on your two versions of the same event. Is there any evidence of misunderstanding or not really listening to each other? Could you have slowed things down, and responded differently?

If miscommunication is an issue

First, decide that in future arguments/upsets you will both take stock and choose to clarify what the other is really saying, rather than jumping to conclusions. Would it help to agree that if either of you isn't quite sure of what the other really means, you will ask. But remember – ask politely and not in an angry or defensive way.

To consider: Would it help to rein in any immediate reactions if you feel upset, angry or hurt – and instead **check things** out? If the other person is trying to be critical this will quickly come out, but at least on occasion you may find that you've both got the wrong end of the stick. Sometimes one of you may be more prone to this, for example when you are tired or after having a drink.

How to notice and respond differently when we feel irritable

i **What pushes your buttons?**

Often, the same frustrating situations or conversations get us feeling irritated and angry again and again. If we can work out what pushes, our buttons, we can then start to consider how to respond differently.

Here are some common situations that can push people's buttons, and make them feel angry and annoyed:

- Your partner putting things in the *'wrong'* place again and again.

- Or doing things the *'wrong'* way – such as stacking the dishwasher or changing the toilet roll.

- People around you are untidy – or more tidy – than you feel is necessary.

- Having different levels of activity – and not liking – or able to do – some of the activities your partner wishes.

- Things people say that annoy such as *'If I were you …'* direct criticisms or correcting the way we do something implying we've got it wrong or, don't do it well enough.

- Too much to do, and feeling under pressure because we can't get through things as quickly, easily and efficiently as when we were younger.

- Having worries on our mind. Not sleeping, not having enough money to pay bills.

- Feeling embarrassed, that we aren't as independent as before or don't understand how to use new technology like the TV box, mobile phone, tablet or computer or keeping up around the house or garden.

- People talking over us or stepping in and taking over decisions we want to make.

 What pushes your own buttons? Write them below:

_____

_____

ii **Watch for your early warning signs.**

We are used to having a smoke or fire alarm in our home to alert us to danger signs. In the same way, the *altered feelings* and *altered physical sensations* in our bodies can act as an early warning system that anger is starting to build.

Things like:

- Feeling hotter or starting to sweat.

- Noticing our heart and breathing rates speeding up.

- Noticing tension in our body starting to rise.

- Being aware of changes in our posture or actions towards the other person. For example raising our voice, standing up, pointing fingers, staring the person down or adopting a more threatening pose.

 What are your own early warning signs of anger rising? Write them below:

_____

_____

iii Choose to respond differently

Once you've noticed the patterns of what pushes your buttons or become aware of any early warning signs, you have a choice of how to respond. In the past, perhaps anger built and led to arguments or upsets. Instead, now you know what's happening, you could instead choose to:

- Leave – walk away and calm things down (*'Let's talk about this later…'*)

- Acknowledge a difference of opinions and respect both viewpoints. Suggest you both take time to reflect on what you do to resolve, this and meet about it at a planned later time.

- Keep sitting down. Sometimes when tensions rise it's tempting to stand up, but this can make things worse if it is misinterpreted that you are being aggressive.

- Count to ten, control your breathing and drop your shoulders to help calm you down.

List your preferred responses. Include any other actions you have noticed have helped before. Write them below:

_____

_____

Why not try this approach, and build skills in controlling your anger?

Violence and threats of violence

If you or a family member is being abused, read this section

Men, women and children – including older adults – can be victims of abuse. It often leads to feelings of shame and isolation. If there is violence toward you or anyone else in the family then you need to be clear this is unacceptable. **If you or your adult child or grandchildren are being threatened or hit** you should think about leaving home – or ask your partner to leave if they are hitting out. Any violence or aggression is unacceptable.

Many people feel powerless in violent relationships – or too scared to leave. If you are in this situation, you should seek professional help, for example talking to your doctor, or contacting social services or the police. If you are scared to do this, tell a trusted friend and go with them. One thing you can be certain about is that unless things change, things are likely to move from bad to worse.

See your phonebook or online for the numbers of your **local domestic violence helplines** and support agencies. These are confidential and can give good advice.

If you yourself are hitting/harming your partner or family member

You need to recognise that hitting/harming your partner or family member is unacceptable. Sometimes this may be new behaviour as a result of anger linked to your depression or tension. Sometimes it's an effect of drink, or a result of reduced inhibitions after stroke or other conditions causing changes to your brain. Or, perhaps violence and threats may be something that you have done for a long time. It's important that you recognise that you are hurting the people whom you love and must stop. Look for times when you are prone to losing control (for example when you are drinking) and tackle this by seeking medical advice and support.

You may find it helpful to join an anger management group. Your doctor can give you more information about this. Reducing how much you drink can help and so can getting treatment for any depression or anxiety. You may find that you will feel better for it – and you may be able to save and rebuild your relationship, too.

Sometimes you need professional advice such as couple counselling to help rebuild your relationship.

Elder abuse

Sometimes adult children may become frustrated with their older parents. Elder abuse, including misuse of your money, property or other resources can be an issue for some. Again, it's important you reach out to other trusted family members, friends and the Police for help.

KEY POINT

Ultimately, although many relationships can be rebuilt or lived with, sometimes they can't, and a time apart or permanent separation even when you've been together a long time may be needed.

SUMMARY

In this workbook you have:

* Reviewed your own style of communicating with others.

* Learned how to build (and rebuild) close relationships with the people around you.

Discovered a three-step approach to controlling anger.

You might want to read or re-read the *Being assertive* workbook about the 'broken record' and 'saying no' approaches and try to practice using them during the next week. In particular, the 'saying no' approach allows you to plan out how to be assertive in a particular situation and with a specific person. View this as an action plan that can help you to both change how you are and also learn something new about yourself and other people.

If relationships are a problem for you, consider showing this workbook to your partner. Read it through together. You might also want to go through the *Information for families and friends – How can you offer the best support* workbook as well.

Worksheets to help you practice

Practice is important to help you master this approach. You can get free access to additional worksheets used in this workbook chapter and the wider book at www.llttf.com/resources

Acknowledgements

The cartoon illustrations were produced by Keith Chan, kchan75@hotmail.com. Thank you to Mrs Theresa Kelly and Mrs Sue Wood at Five Areas Ltd for their helpful advice and comments on earlier drafts of this book. Also, to those practitioners and Peer mentors at North West Senior and Disability Services in Oregon, USA who inputted into the initial modifications of these resources to suit an older adult readership.

Overcoming Depression and Low Mood in Older Adults

A Five Areas® CBT Approach

Information for families and friends

How can you offer the best support?

Dr Chris Williams

DOI: 10.4324/9781003347637-8

Do you ever notice this?

Is this your situation?

If so, … this workbook is for you.

This workbook is for family and friends of older adults who are experiencing low mood or depression. It also tells you more about the *Overcoming depression and low mood for older adults* resources, so that family and friends can understand and offer support in the best possible way.

In this workbook you will learn about:

• What this course is about – and how the person is using it.

• Helpful things you can do so that you can offer the support that the person needs.

• Unhelpful things that you should try not to do which can undermine the support you can give.

• Looking after yourself as a friend or relative so that you stay well.

• Putting what you've learned into practice.

Background for friends and family

The course workbooks use a tried and tested approach based on cognitive behavioural therapy (CBT, a kind of talking treatment). CBT can work well for people who are facing problems in their lives – including stress and low mood. Research on a different version of this book used by adults across the age range has found that using the book with support can be an effective aid for depression.

An important part of your role as a carer is to help encourage the person you are supporting and keep them on track while they try to work on their problems.

The approach used in the course helps the reader look at the impact of low mood or anxiety on five important areas of life. The Five Areas® Assessment helps a person recognise the kinds of problems they may be facing in each of the following areas:

1 The situations, relationships and practical problems involving the people and events around them.

2 Their thinking (identifying any unhelpful thinking that makes them feel worse).

3 Their feelings (emotions).

4 Their altered physical symptoms and sensations. This also takes into account that many older people are also living with long-term physical health problems such as heart, lung problems, post-stroke and more.

5 Their behaviour (typically with reduced activity levels due to low mood, or avoidance because of anxiety).

KEY POINT

Figure 6.1 shows that what we think about a situation or problem may affect how we feel emotionally and physically. It can also unhelpfully alter what we do.

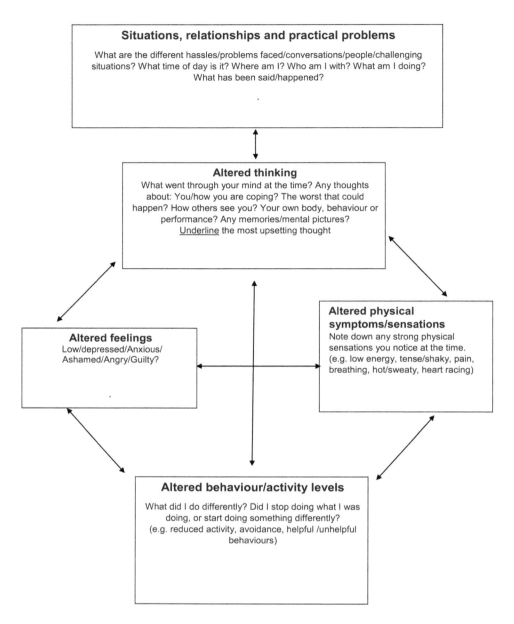

Figure 6.1 The Five Areas® Assessment

Because of the two-way links between each of the Five Areas®, it means that making helpful changes in any one of the areas can lead to benefits in the other areas as well. Finally, it means that **the people around the person can also help change things.**

About the workbook approach

This workbook is one of a many within the *Overcoming depression and low mood in older adults* book. Each is designed to be worked through when a topic is relevant to the person or their situation.

They:

- Provide useful information about how low mood affects someone's life.

- Teach important life skills to help make changes in order to feel better.

They are practical **work**books that encourage the person to apply them, not just read them. Although some of the principles can seem easy – they can be hard to apply again and again in life so practice, and encouragement from family and friends is often helpful.

The workbooks are usually used one at a time – and the reader is encouraged to read them slowly. This allows them to practice what they have learned before moving on to the next one. The person can discuss the workbooks (if they want) with others such as family members, friends, or a healthcare practitioner. Each workbook is their own resource and is private to them. Some people find it helpful to share them – but you need to respect their wishes. The workbooks are like someone's personal diary and in the same way they aren't meant to be read by everyone.

However, this particular workbook is designed to be read and discussed jointly.

How can you help?

Your role is to try and offer **supportive encouragement**. This means:

- Being interested.

- Being hopeful as well as realistic.

- Encouraging the person to try things out –even if he/she feels bad at the time.

- Suggesting or freeing up a time when they can use the materials. For example you can help by answering the phone and the door for an hour or so.

- Encouraging not badgering. Ultimately, the person has to choose to do things they value and see as important to them.

- Asking how you can help. Some people prefer to work alone or with someone independent such as a health or voluntary sector worker.

It's important to remember that you are a friend or relative and not a therapist. Let the workbooks do the teaching and the educational work. Your role is to help encourage your relative or friend to read the materials and try out the suggested activities.

Other ways of supporting – keeping talking

A common problem that happens when someone is struggling, is that their family or friends may not fully understand what is happening or know how to offer help. Seeing each other's point of view at times like this is important. The danger is when either party starts to think that those around them no longer care. Stating clearly what you are thinking and feeling can really help.

Low mood or depression is more likely to occur when chronic illness is present. This includes chronic pain such as arthritis, diabetes, heart disease, stroke, mobility issues, deafness or stroke. Focusing on what the individual has to say is important whatever the disability or age.

You may have all sorts of other worries. You may be concerned about the reactions of other people to your friend or relative's problem. For example the attitude and comments of a spouse, neighbours, colleagues, healthcare practitioners, people at their place of worship and other friends or relatives. It could be when you've tried to help, you were uncertain how best to do this. You may struggle to know what to say. If you feel that you can't talk through how things are – or are unsure how either of you can show that you care – going through this workbook together may help.

Understanding the causes of low mood and depression

When a person breaks his/her leg, there is usually a large plaster cast on the leg to see. This is easily seen. But some symptoms aren't so visible. For example problems of tiredness, weakness, dizziness and pain decreasing mobility or physical ability. The same is true of feelings of sadness, stress and tension which again aren't visible in the same way as a broken leg, heart disease or cancer. Like high blood pressure or sugar levels, the problem is there, and has serious impacts and is important to treat. Yet you often can't see it in quite the same way as other more visible issues.

Some relatives and friends find they just can't understand how someone can become depressed. They may think that there's no reason why depression should occur. But remember that depression can affect anyone if enough life challenges coincide. There are lots of different reasons – physical, psychological, social – why a person can start to feel low in mood. Even 'happy' events such as a holiday or having a new grandchild can bring unexpected pressures. The important thing is that whatever the cause of your friend or relative's depression, you are there to help.

How to offer effective help

Now complete the following checklist. It will help you recognise your friend or relative's strengths and identifies possible problems that you may wish to tackle together. You might find it helpful to first go through the checklist separately and then discuss your answers to each question together.

Can you identify any of these common problems that can arise?

Q Does your friend or relative find it hard to talk to and receive support from others?

Yes ☐   No ☐   Sometimes ☐

Q Is there anyone around they can talk to? Perhaps they have moved, or friends/family have moved away, or died?

Yes ☐   No ☐   Sometimes ☐

Q Are you or others unsure how to best offer support?

Yes ☐   No ☐   Sometimes ☐

Q Are you or others avoiding talking about important symptoms and their impact?

Yes ☐   No ☐   Sometimes ☐

Q Is your healthcare practitioners struggling to offer the right support in treating symptoms?

Yes ☐   No ☐   Sometimes ☐

Q Are their symptoms not 'visible' or obvious to others?

Yes ☐   No ☐   Sometimes ☐

If Yes, does this seem to affect how others react?

Yes ☐   No ☐   Sometimes ☐

Write down what you have both noticed here:

_____

_____

Avoiding things

When people feel anxious or worried about things, they can avoid situations such as other people, places, activities or even conversations that they think may be difficult or stressful. This adds to their problems because although they may feel less anxious or unwell in the shorter term. In the longer term, such actions can worsen the problem.

KEY POINT

Avoidance teaches that the only way of dealing with a difficult situation is by avoiding it. Avoidance reduces opportunities to discover that our worst fears don't occur. It worsens anxiety and strongly undermines confidence.

EXAMPLE: Anne and Mary's vicious circles of avoidance

Anne has arthritis and has been struggling to cope with her symptoms for several years. She finds it difficult to keep up with things in her apartment or to get out and about.

Over the past few months, Anne has felt increasingly depressed. Her confidence has taken a huge knock and she can no longer cope with things. She tends to sit indoors – and cries from time to time. Her symptoms continue to worsen and now she also feels she cannot enjoy things that she used to. Anne's sister, Mary, lives on the other side of town and likes to drop by once every week or so. A big problem for Anne is that she feels very embarrassed when things aren't clean and neat in her flat and when she isn't nicely dressed.

So, now, whenever Mary comes by, Anne feels uneasy that Mary will notice that she isn't coping. She feels deeply ashamed of how things are and becomes very upset. This is illustrated in Figure 6.2a.

Mary is also concerned about Anne. She knows that Anne isn't herself. Mary wants to speak to Anne about how she wants to help. But as a family, they have always struggled to be open about how they feel. Although they know they care for each other, this isn't something that would usually be said. Now whenever Mary visits Anne, she sits thinking, 'We should be discussing things – how can

I help'? She has tried to bring up her concerns once or twice, but Anne quickly becomes defensive and seems embarrassed. This is illustrated in Figure 6.2b.

Both Anne and Mary think, 'What can we do?'

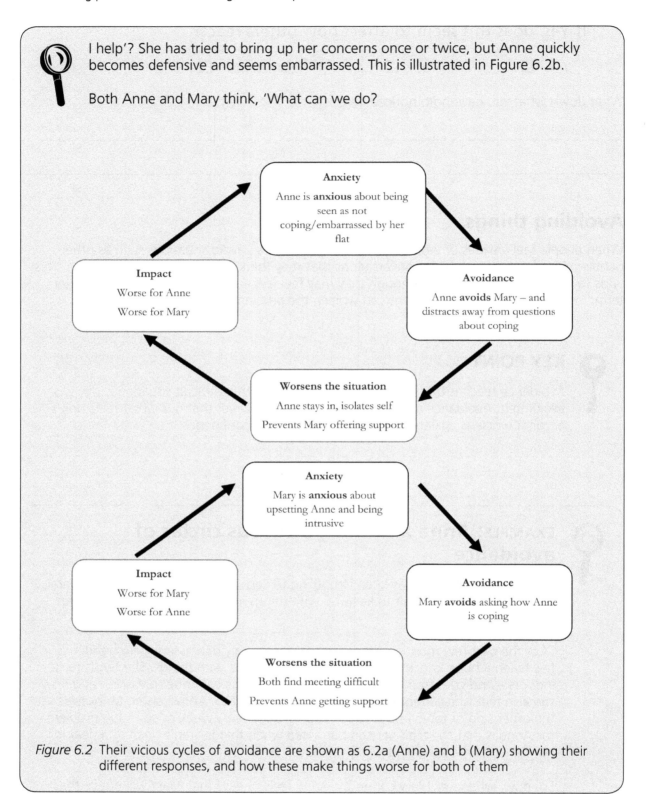

Figure 6.2 Their vicious cycles of avoidance are shown as 6.2a (Anne) and b (Mary) showing their different responses, and how these make things worse for both of them

Now consider the questions below.

Q   **How are Anne and Mary's reactions making the situation worse?**

_____

_____

Q   **What could they do to change things?**

_____

_____

As the example shows, sometimes, even just talking about the symptoms can become something to be avoided at home or with friends. Even among close relatives and friends, a person may feel embarrassed about discussing such things.

The checklist below describes some common areas of avoidance you might fall into as a carer/supporter

As a friend/family member, are you:	Check here if you have noticed this – even if just sometimes
Avoiding asking anything about low mood or anxiety?	☐
Avoiding talking to anyone else about your friend or relative's symptoms or about how they are coping?	☐
Putting off all decisions for the future. For example putting holidays or other life plans completely on hold.	☐
Not really being honest. For example saying 'Yes' when you really mean 'No'?	☐
Trying hard to avoid situations that bring about upsetting thoughts/memories?	☐
Not arranging activities with your own friends or alone – and therefore no longer living your own life to the full?	☐
Avoiding discussing how you yourself are feeling or coping?	☐
Not seeing people that are good for you/or actively isolating yourself from others?	☐
Avoiding expressing concerns about how others in the family are doing even when you've noticed they are struggling?	☐
Avoiding being assertive about your own needs?	☐
Avoiding going out in public either by yourself or with the person you are supporting? (Perhaps finding walking, or walking speed or use of accessories such as wheelchairs clumsy, hard or embarrassing)?	☐
Avoiding being at home: keeping so busy that you don't have to think about the problem?	☐
For partners/spouses: if you are the person's partner/ spouse, are you avoiding sex or physical intimacy? Perhaps you have fears of causing over-exertion or harm? Or perhaps you're not sure whether this would be imposing/ inappropriate or not wanted at present?	☐

Are you avoiding things in other ways?

If this is so, write down here what you are avoiding:

_____

_____

Sometimes, some of these questions can be hard to discuss. This may especially be so around issues such as sex or intimacy. You can always decide to discuss them at a later time but don't ignore them as they are important.

Remember that at times the avoidance can be quite subtle. For example choosing to steer conversations away from difficult areas that would actually benefit from being discussed. Often people fear upsetting the other person or making them feel worse. This can backfire, however, because it means issues aren't dealt with.

The need for clear communication

The only way of overcoming avoidance is through openness and honesty. Without this, many problems can arise. If you are someone who worries about hurting other people's feelings or aren't quite sure how to discuss these things openly, then you might find the *Being assertive* and *Building relationships with your family and friends* workbooks helpful.

Here are some practical phrases and strategies you can use to relate differently to each other.

- *'This isn't a good time to talk, let's talk about it later'*, – if you make sure you do.

- Sometimes people need to work through an issue by talking at length. Let them talk, often no comment is needed. Listen for the main message and then pick up on this point so the person knows you are really listening. For example *'It sounds like you feel frustrated/fed up today'*.

- Offer praise and encouragement to build confidence, for example *'I can see such a difference from a month ago'*.

- Actively look for things you can comment positively about (*e.g. 'That dress looks really nice on you'* or *'The grandchildren really enjoyed playing that game with you'*.

- Try to find at least three encouraging or thankful things to say every day.

Helpful and unhelpful responses

When someone you care about needs your help, most people try to improve things. Mostly, our responses are likely to be helpful. Sometimes, however – without meaning to, how we react can become unhelpful.

This section focuses on both the helpful and possibly unhelpful behaviours that friends, relatives, caregivers may do.

Helpful supports by family and friends

- Find out about depression, for example by reading the workbooks in this course. Or read other information resources from credible organisations such as nationally recognised self-help groups or from healthcare practitioners. This can equip you with the knowledge and skills you need.

- 'Being there' for the person over the long term.

- Being willing to talk and offer support when needed.

- Listening when the person talks, sometimes he/she just wants to talk and does not expect the listener to fix things.

- Asking questions of experts such as their GP, therapist or practitioner.

- Encouraging the person to put what they are learning through the book resources into practice.

- Realising there are no quick fixes.

- Using your sense of humour to help you and the person you support to cope.

- Seeing a healthcare practitioner for advice if you, yourself, are struggling to cope.

- Recovering from depression takes time. Even when mood improves, there is a period of weeks to months where a person is more vulnerable to relapse. Think about a broken leg. When the plaster comes off, you wouldn't expect them to run a marathon the next day! Muscles need to be built up again. In the same way, although the depression may lift, a person needs to build up their confidence and activities slowly again. Helping them plan their activities is one of the best ways of reducing the risk of relapse.

 ## Are you doing anything else that is helpful?

 ### KEY POINT

The hallmark of a truly helpful activity is that it's good for you and usually for others as well.

Unhelpful behaviours by family and friends

Most carers look to provide helpful support. However, that support can sometimes become unhelpful.

Two commonly seen unhelpful patterns of support are:

i **Wrapping the person in cotton wool – sometimes called emotional-over-involvement**

Here, the motive is to protect the older person who is being supported. This is done by stepping in and making all decisions. So, if someone wants to walk through to the kitchen to make a cup of tea, they are told 'I'll do that'. The same might occur if they want to walk or drive to the local shops. Or perhaps you visit the doctor or physiotherapist or other medical appointment with them. When they are asked about their symptoms, you might be tempted to jump in and answer on their behalf, correcting them or talking over your relative as you make sure the professional gets an accurate story. While well-meaning these supportive actions can seem frustrating and too controlling for your relative.

Perhaps they have lived a lifetime when they have been able to make decisions and run their own house. Or they know they need to keep moving to keep their muscles and joints working well and being told to sit still while someone else takes over isn't what they need.

The solution isn't to do nothing, but it does raise the issue of what can we do that really helps? Sometimes some extra help carrying or getting things can be useful. But so can going for a walk together.

Again, sometimes it can be helpful letting professionals such as GP's know if your relative is struggling. But picking the right time when they have told their story and asking if you could add something is important.

>
> **KEY POINT**
>
> If you are tempted to step in and say – 'Don't do that' or 'I'll do this' – stop and think if it is reducing your relatives' capacity and confidence. If so, instead, try and ask – 'how can I help'?

Q Am I prone to wrapping the person I care for in cotton wool?

Yes ☐   No ☐   Sometimes ☐

Q Am I someone who takes overall responsibility from the person?

Yes ☐   No ☐   Sometimes ☐

Q Do I encourage them to avoid doing things because of fears about what harm might result? For example taking over going to shops or taking on all the driving?

Yes ☐   No ☐   Sometimes ☐

Q Do I speak for/over the person in social settings or in a hospital outpatient area, etc.?

Yes ☐   No ☐   Sometimes ☐

Q Do I make all the important decisions or try to control every aspect of their life?

Yes ☐   No ☐   Sometimes ☐

Q Have I taken over all activities they used to do, so they don't have to 'worry' about them?

Yes ☐   No ☐   Sometimes ☐

ii **Being overly critical and letting your frustration come through**

It can be hard being a carer. It may stop you taking holidays, or going shopping, to the cinema, theatre or to visit friends. Perhaps you've really looked forward to new opportunities when you retire, Or maybe the person you are supporting has changed. Perhaps they have lost confidence because of feeling down, and now seem anxious and scared to do anything. Or maybe they have lost confidence in their walking after a fall, and won't walk far or want someone on both sides of them to feel safe, shouting out if they feel you move in a way that makes them feel unstable and scared they might fall. Or they complain all the time about taking tablets, or struggle to swallow larger tablets, or food, and want you to constantly reassure them about one thing after another.

We can all generally help support someone who struggles for a few days or even a few weeks. But it can become so much harder when this becomes a longer time period. Even if we are usually calm, loving and supportive, it's possible that with time, tiredness and frustration, that we can become irritated. If that irritation comes out as critical comments or saying nasty things in a nasty way, it can worsen the situation even more by making their depression worse. For example some people may find that raising their voice in frustration can make them feel a lot better to begin with. But this can have a damaging effect on your relationship and leave you feeling guilty.

Q **At times am I letting my frustration out by saying critical comments in a nasty way?**

Yes ☐   No ☐   Sometimes ☐

If you have replied *Yes* or *Sometimes* to either of these questions or to any of the questions, we recommend you talk this over with the person you support.

The next section of this workbook will help you identify areas of support you could work on together.

Other unhelpful responses

No matter how helpful something may seem to begin with, if taken to an extreme most responses can backfire. For example, seeking support from others is sensible. Sharing a problem can really help – but if you find that your friend or relative is constantly on the phone **seeking reassurance** – and feels they can't cope without talking to others, then something that was originally helpful, has become a problem.

Other unhelpful behaviours include:

• Offering '*helpful advice*' **all the time**.

• A desire to do **everything** for the person.

• **Constantly** offering reassurance that everything will work out fine ('*Of course you'll be okay*').

You can see that the words in bold here make this same point again. The motive may be good and some of these actions may be helpful to some extent. But when taken to excess, they become unhelpful.

There are many reasons why people behave in this way. Often, it's due to concern, friendship and love. Sometimes it may be the result of anxiety or occasionally guilt. Whatever the cause, when people offer too much help and want to do everything for someone else, their actions can backfire and worsen things.

Frustration and anger at healthcare practitioners

It isn't unusual that when someone takes on a supportive or caregiver role that they can struggle themselves. Different feelings such as discouragement, worry, guilt, frustration or even anger can occur. These frustrations can spill over into how you talk about healthcare practitioners. It can be tempting to become critical. Most healthcare practitioners can offer helpful support to people. But from time to time, even those working in the caring professions may not be able to offer the kind of support that you feel your friend or relative needs.

KEY POINT

If you are too critical of healthcare practitioners, there is a danger that you will undermine the support and advice that they can offer.

But what if you disagree?

Sometimes people have strong opinions about what treatments or investigations their friend or relative may need. For example, a person may have strong opinions about **alternative** and **complementary** medicine approaches, or just happy that the current treatment is working. They may have understandable worries about medication, especially for an older person.

If your friend or relative is being offered treatments or tests that you have concerns about, it's important to be aware of how you are responding. If they have been prescribed medication, try not to persuade them to suddenly stop taking this without discussing this with their doctor. If you have strong concerns that a treatment is wrong or not needed, it's best for you both to go (if the person who is unwell is okay with this) to their doctor to discuss things. What all of you want is the best possible outcome.

Automatically advising the person not to try recommended treatment approaches because of your fears that it may do harm?	☐
Undermining or criticising healthcare practitioners? (Perhaps because they haven't been able to find a cure.)	☐
Constantly asking about how they are? (Which can unhelpfully draw attention to illness or disability.)	☐

Some other areas of life that can become affected by unhelpful responses

Consider your responses to the following questions.

Are you: Becoming so focused on the distressed person that other people's needs aren't met? (For example your own or other family members such as grandchildren are overlooked.).	☐
Depending on or needing the sufferer to be well and functioning? (So that they aren't allowed to be unwell.)	☐
Making snap decisions about important issues? For example resigning a post to look after the person.	☐
Constantly reassuring the person to calm their anxious fears?	☐
Constantly asking about how they are? (Which can unhelpfully draw attention to illness or disability).	☐

Q Write down any other unhelpful behaviours here:

_____

_____

Q Overall: what effect do any unhelpful behaviours have on you both?

_____

_____

The problem is that these responses can quickly become a habit – where the same pattern is repeated again and again.

Faith and seeking help

Caregivers may sometimes have a strong spiritual belief. They may find this very helpful, but sometimes these beliefs can emphasise prayer as the **only** way toward recovery and healing.

People may overlook that therapists may be an important part of the recovery process and they may be part of an answer to prayer. In the same way that you would recommend someone seeks medical help if they broke their arm or leg, the person needs to seek appropriate help for severe low mood and depression. If you have doubts about how medical help, a talking therapy or counselling can help low mood and depression, please discuss this with a spiritual leader whom you respect.

Looking after yourself

When you support others, you also need to look after yourself and allow time and space for your own needs. Depression and stress are very common among caregivers. The danger is that you are so busy offering support that you have no time for yourself. Most relatives want to help when an older relative or friend struggles. At the same time, it's important to decide what level of help you are able to offer. Perhaps you live far away? Or is someone living nearer than other potential supporters and seems the obvious person to help when an older relative struggles? Or perhaps you are a spouse or partner living in the same house or flat? It can be difficult sometimes finding a balance between the support you offer, while also looking after your own needs for space, time, work and times to recharge. There are no right or wrong levels of support. Sometimes someone may need more support when they especially struggle – for example with physical illness. At times like this, perhaps the NHS or social services can help provide additional support, or this could be considered via a private agency if funds allow.

It can help to be clear about what you can and can't offer. Also, to plan gaps when you as a carer or supporter can have time off, or time away. The term **respite care** describes the situation where your friend or relative is able to move temporarily into a hotel, residential or nursing home for a short time, to allow you/a carer to get away, or have a gap to recharge. Sometimes carers feel very guilty even considering doing this. However, it's important to have periods like this, as carer depression and potentially burnout might leave the person needing support in a worse situation if a key carer is suddenly not available for weeks or longer.

Are you:

Q **Planning time for yourself as well as for others.**

Yes ☐   No ☐   Sometimes ☐

Q **Using effective coping strategies to deal with your own feelings of tension.**

Yes ☐   No ☐   Sometimes ☐

Q **Looking after yourself.**

Yes ☐   No ☐   Sometimes ☐

Responses that will help you look after yourself include:

- Open discussion about your own stress – for example with your own doctor or perhaps within a caregiver support group.

- Taking short breaks or getaways.

- Planning 'me time' such as engaging hobbies/interests/night classes.

- Attending caregiver support groups.

Where to get extra help

Ideally, the older person with depression has someone like you to support them during their depression. But there are times when this won't be enough. You should support your friend or relative to get extra help if you think they have any of the following signs or symptoms:

- **Severe depression**, for example continuing low mood, tearfulness, a serious lack of sleep or concentration or a marked loss of weight or energy despite attempts to improve things.

- Urges to **self-harm** or feeling really **hopeless** or experiencing **suicidal** thoughts.

- Other **dangerous behaviours**, for example: risk-taking, behaviours like speeding through red lights or threats of harm to others.

- A possibility of immediate or longer-term significant harm or injury by someone else. For example, observed or suspected **abuse or neglect by personal caregivers including concerns for the health or safety of your friend or relative**.

- **Severe withdrawal from life activities**, for example they are clearly not coping well and stop going grocery shopping.

- **Serious weight** loss or the person has **stopped drinking fluids** so they become dry and dehydrated.

There could be other situations as well where extra help is needed or can be a real help. If in doubt, it's important to ask for help in deciding whether more support is needed.

If there is a risk of immediate significant harm (abuse, self-harm or suicide), urgent action will need to be taken immediately. Phone for an ambulance/emergency services. Remember that professional and voluntary services can give a great deal of support.

What if the person doesn't agree they need extra help?

It is always best to get the person's agreement for getting extra help, but sometimes the risks involved may mean help is needed whether they agree or not.

If you are seriously worried that extra help is needed but the person is refusing, it's still best to ask for help in deciding if anything else should or can be done. Contact an area social services agency or ask your doctor. You can discuss the issues in confidence and will receive sensible advice as to what you should do.

KEY POINT

If you are still worried or concerned, it is better to ask for help or advice than do nothing.

SUMMARY

In this workbook you have learned:

- What this course is about – and how your friend or relative is using it.

- How to help and communicate effectively.

- Helpful and unhelpful things you can do so that you can offer effective support.

- How to look after yourself and stay well.

Before you go

What have you learned from this workbook?

_____

_____

What do you want to try next?

_____

_____

 Think about how you can put what you've learned into your own life. If you recognise that there are changes you need – or you both need to make, try to:

• Choose just one or two areas to work on first.

• Make a clear plan of what you can do differently, and when you can do it.

• Communicate with each other. Ask for what you need. Be straightforward and honest with each other.

Worksheets to help you practice

Practice is important to help you master this approach. You can get free access to additional worksheets used in this workbook chapter and the wider book at www.llttf.com/resources

Acknowledgements

The cartoon illustrations were produced by Keith Chan, kchan75@hotmail.com. Thank you to Mrs Theresa Kelly and Mrs Sue Wood at Five Areas Ltd for their helpful advice and comments on earlier drafts of this book. Also, to those practitioners and Peer mentors at North West Senior and Disability Services in Oregon, USA who inputted into the initial modifications of these resources to suit an older adult readership.

The term Five Areas® is a registered trademark of Five Areas Resources Ltd. Although we hope you find this book helpful, it's not intended to be a direct substitute for consultative advice with a healthcare professional, nor do we give any assurance about its effectiveness in a particular case. Accordingly, neither we nor the author shall be held liable for any loss or damages arising from its use.

PART 3

Making changes to what you do

Overcoming Depression and Low Mood in Older Adults

A Five Areas® CBT Approach

Doing things that make you feel better

Dr Chris Williams

DOI: 10.4324/9781003347637-10

Do you ever notice this?

Is this you?

If so, ... this workbook is for you.

In this workbook you will learn about:

- How low mood and stress cause you to do less.

- How reduced activity and avoidance affect you.

- How to identify things you have cut down or stopped doing which you used to enjoy.

- Which activities help you feel better and consider how to plan these into your life.

- How to build a helpful routine across your day.

Low mood creates inactivity

Low mood and stress make life seem difficult because of:

- Unhelpful thoughts about doing things *'I just can't do it')*. The result is you **say no** to things you might have enjoyed.

- Low energy and tiredness *('I'm so exhausted')* saps your ability to act.

- Low or anxious mood. So, you don't really enjoy things even when you do them.

- Little sense of achievement, so you don't recognise the things you're able to still do.

- Physical health problems which can frustrate and grind you down. Symptoms such as pain, exhaustion or weakness, breathlessness, chest discomfort or dizziness can make it harder to live life than before, and you end up doing less and less.

- Putting off tasks and dealing with problems – which then can build up making you feel even worse.

This reduced activity has an impact on all aspects of our lives.

Inactivity can worsen how you feel emotionally

Many people try to force themselves to do things they feel should/must/ought/have to be done. Activities like looking after grandchildren, working, or volunteering or doing chores. At the same time, **activities they would usually do for fun or friendship are slowly, squeezed out.**

Think about the impact this would have on anyone's life if they slowly removed the things they usually enjoy. Their life would become smaller, and life would lose its colour and variety.

Inactivity can also worsen how you feel physically

As you get older, there is a risk that inactivity causes us to seize up and become stiffer. Also, muscles that haven't been used as much as before can weaken, leaving us feeling frailer. You may notice, if you walk around or go upstairs, your muscles might ache and your heart and breathing race because you've become unfit. That can cause a further vicious cycle where we feel weaker and unsteady on our feet, causing us to avoid getting going again as a result.

A key thing to remember is that activity and movement are good for you and are one of the targets for you to work on in this workbook.

But the good news is that a slow, steady increase in activity can help improve your physical strength, stability and flexibility and, reduce any pain and tiredness you have. This is why physiotherapists and doctors advise people to increase activity levels. It can also boost your mood.

EXAMPLE: Anne's reduced activities.

Anne has arthritis. Until six months ago she regularly walked to the park and sat on her favourite bench, enjoying watching people cycle and walk past. She also loved listening to the radio and reading. She enjoyed seeing her grandchildren. However, they moved away just before she became depressed. She misses them every day, and although they talk on the phone, it isn't the same and she feels lonely.

Over that last six months, Anne has felt increasingly low and upset and noticed worsening pain and stiffness in her hands and joints. She has stopped reading, listening to the radio and going to the park. She sits alone in her chair all day in her flat with the letters piling up unopened at the door. Her back and legs feel stiffer, making it more difficult for her to get out walking. She is now anxious about walking downstairs as she feels weaker, frailer and less secure walking.

Look at the vicious cycle of reduced activity diagram (Figure 7.1) to understand what is happening to Anne.

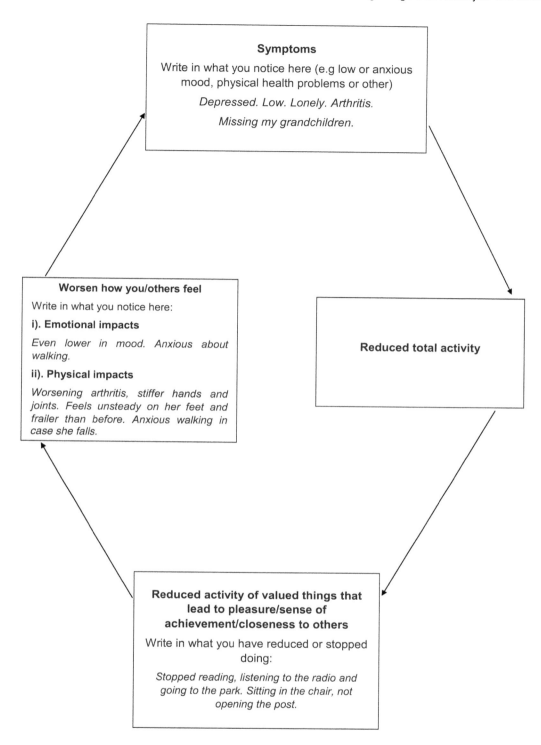

Figure 7.1 Anne's vicious cycle of reduced activity

What about you?

Now think about your own life.

Q **Overall, have you stopped or cut down doing things because of how you feel?**

Yes ☐   No ☐   Sometimes ☐

Q **Has the reduced activity or avoidance removed things from your life that previously gave you pleasure?**

Yes ☐   No ☐   Sometimes ☐

Q **Are you spending less time with people you like such as family/ friends?**

Yes ☐   No ☐   Sometimes ☐

Q **Has the reduced activity or avoidance worsened how you feel physically – making you feel more tired, weaker, stiffer, or less steady walking?**

Yes ☐   No ☐   Sometimes ☐

Q **Have you reduced your own activities? Write what you haven't been doing as much/at all below.**

_____

_____

Inactivity can affect your daily routine

Since things feel harder to do, you may focus on resting and just getting by. This can mean you start to lose the usual structure of your day. All those routine things you took for granted can start to be lost:

- Getting up at a regular time.

- Washing your hair and bathing/showering regularly.

- Eating regular meals, including breakfast and cooking food.

- Going out for walks, such as walking your dog if you have one. Or volunteering/meeting family or friends.

- Going to bed at a regular time. Often when people struggle, they spend more time in bed, sleeping in, or napping during the day.

Things you can do to feel better

Planning and doing certain activities can be good for you emotionally and physically.

First, **rebuild your routine**/pattern to each day. There are several set points to your day. A time to get up, and go to sleep. A time to eat breakfast, lunch and tea/dinner. These key time points can helpfully split each day up. That way, you can plan additional activities you choose to do each morning, afternoon and evening.

Task: Write in the time of day:

I get up at: …………

I have breakfast at: …………

I have lunch at: …………

I have tea/dinner at: …………

I go to bed at: …………

Q **Has your day shifted over time? Are you sleeping in? Or taking extra naps during the day?**

_____

_____

A first target is to shift your day towards a regular pattern where you get up rather than lie listlessly in bed.

Avoid napping – or if you have a snooze make sure it's short.

For the meals, you don't have to eat larger amounts, but it is helpful to eat regularly across the day. Meals provide energy, vitamins, minerals and protein which are important for your muscles and health. You may find that illness and age make you feel you want smaller portions or you pick at food and don't eat it fully. Or maybe you graze and snack with chocolate or favourite cakes and treats throughout the day, meaning you feel less hungry at meal times.

Dieticians can advise on what you eat. They can also advise if you have particular **problems swallowing**. Also consider your exercise routine – and what is possible for you based on your body, strength and other illnesses. Being active around your home and garden can be part of maintaining your strength balance and flexibility. Physiotherapists, falls clinics and exercise classes might all be things to consider for advice and support. **Using small weight** (e.g. 1kg) to strengthen your arms can be used while you watch television or sit. **Standing up regularly** and walking can be very helpful. If this is impossible or difficult, just do what you can. Perhaps set a clock or alarm to prompt you. If you are able to, exercises to improve balance and stability might be useful. Age UK (www.ageuk.org.uk) and other large charities and the NHS are good sources of advice as to what might be appropriate and safe for you.

Choosing which activities to do

First, you need to identify some potential activities to plan to do. Have a look through the list below and tick the ones that apply to you. Good choices include things you used to enjoy, but have cut down on or stopped doing because of how you feel.

Checklist of reduced/avoided activities:

As a result of how you feel, are you:	Tick here if you have noticed changes – even if just sometimes
Getting up and going to bed at irregular times?	☐
Stopping or reducing doing hobbies, or other things you previously enjoyed or did to relax?	☐
Going out or meeting friends less than usual?	☐
Eating poorly (e.g. eating much less or eating more snacks, chocolate and cake)?	☐
Noticing physical consequences of reduced activity – such as worsened pain or restricted joint movement?	☐
Just sitting watching TV?	☐
Not volunteering or doing things that you value and see as important, such as helping others?	☐
Failing to keep up with housework (are you 'letting things go' around the house)?	☐
Avoiding people or conversations that seem stressful?	
Not always answering the phone or the door when people visit?	☐
Putting off the essentials, such as leaving letters/bills unopened or not replying to them?	☐
Paying less attention to your self-care (e.g. bathing less, less bothered about your appearance, not shaving)?	☐
Stopping/cutting down on gardening – perhaps then feeling distressed when you look at the long grass or weeds?	☐
Avoiding places or activities that seem scary/challenging or too much to handle?	
Playing a musical instrument/singing/choir? Or listening/enjoying live or recorded music?	☐
Reading a good book/magazine or watching a movie?	☐
Are you less interested in sex (e.g. pushing your partner away because of a lack of enjoyment/energy for sex)?	☐
Staying inactive so that you are far less physically active than before?	☐
If you have a religious faith: have you reduced or stopped reading your Holy Book, praying or going to your place of worship?	☐

Choosing a first target

From your list above, you may have identified several activities you have reduced or stopped.

It isn't possible to overcome all these areas at once. You need to decide on **one** activity to concentrate on to start with. Pick an activity that is likely to make a helpful impact, and can be easily planned into your life.

My first activity to target is:

_____

_____

Making activity manageable

The all-or-nothing approach

Overdoing things can sometimes be just as unhelpful as under-doing things.

This is called the **all-or-nothing** response. The person overly throws themselves into things on days when they feel better, then later they crash back. So, on average over time they do less and less.

For example if you are ironing the clothes:

Taking a planned approach would include a break halfway through and maybe finishing later that day.

Taking an **'all-or-nothing'** approach would mean that you throw yourself into doing it all at once – exhausting yourself in the process.

EXAMPLE:

Tom is in his late seventies and lives alone. He has moved into a flat from a larger family home with a garden after his wife died. He ticks several boxes in the checklist of activities including just sitting watching TV. He realises this is a pattern he's got stuck in. He decides he will change this around and next day goes out for a **long walk** alone to explore the local area. He really struggles on the return journey and feels quite unwell as he gets home. He went to bed and didn't have anything to eat that evening. The next morning, he wakes up feeling tired and achy. He doesn't fancy doing another walk and goes back to watching the TV. Instead of enjoying the walk and building his fitness slowly, the initial overly long walk was too much.

Breaking activities down into smaller steps

Some smaller activities can be planned easily. However, some may need more planning. For some activities, you may need to break down your target into many **smaller steps** that you can tackle one at a time. So, to go to the cinema with friends, you might need to decide who to ask, check what film is showing, decide which one to go to, get there and back, etc. You can plan any stages of this you want to using this approach.

Q **Do you need to break your own target down into something more realistic and achievable?**

Yes ☐   or   No? ☐

If so, re-write what you want to do:

My updated first step is:

_____

_____

Next, make a plan to do it

You need to have a clear plan that states exactly **what** you are going to do and **when** you are going to do it. Another important part of the plan is to predict what could block the plan.

 TOM'S EXAMPLE:

Tom, reads this workbook, and realises his all or nothing thinking led him to over-commit. The result was that something that could have been fun has become an off-putting burden. He decides to try again, but to start with something shorter.

Tom's revised plan:

What am I going to do:

I'll walk to the local shop which is about ten minutes away.

When am I going to do it:

Tomorrow at 10 am.

Is my planned task useful for understanding or changing how I am?

Yes – it will get me moving, and I fancy finding somewhere to sit down and read the paper to give me a rest before coming home.

Clear and specific, so that I will know when I have done it?

Yes – I'll know by 11 am tomorrow if I've done it.

Realistic, practical and achievable?

Yes, it's not too far. I'll look to see if there is somewhere to buy my shopping. It would be good to have a coffee before coming back.

What problems or difficulties could arise – and how could I overcome these?

I could forget – so I'll set a reminder in my phone. It might rain – well I'm waterproof and have a coat and umbrella.

Tom then acts on his plan: Tom walks to the local shops and sits down for a cup of coffee while he reads the paper in a local café. He does this for several days running and starts to have short conversations with the café staff which he enjoys.

What about you? Write your own plan here:

1 **What am I going to do?**

_____

2 **When am I going to do it?**

_____

3 **IS MY PLANNED TASK:**

_____

Q Useful for understanding or changing how I am?

Yes ☐   No ☐

Q Clear and specific, so that I will know when I have done it?

Yes ☐   No ☐

Q Realistic, practical and achievable?

Yes ☐   No ☐

Q What problems or difficulties could arise – and how could I overcome these?

_____

_____

Now, carry out your plan

Try to do your plan anyway. Good luck!

My Review of how it went

Afterwards, even if it went well, stop and reflect on how things went. If things didn't go as you wanted, try to stop, think and reflect so you can learn from this. That way you can put what you're learning into practice so you make better and better plans going forward.

• What went well?

• What didn't go so well?

• How can you take what you've learned so you make better and better plans going forward?

Now write down your own review:

_____

_____

_____

What if symptoms get in the way?

It's quite common to find that when it comes to doing a task, you might be tempted to put it off (*'I'll do it next week'* or talk yourself out of it. Perhaps you might feel worse at the time, maybe tired, lower in mood, more negative or fed-up. Or it rains or is cold outside.

If that's the case, then choose to change what you say to yourself.

Instead of saying *'I was going to do it, but I felt really tired/stiff/down/fed up/anxious'*, …

Change it to: *"I'm going to choose to do it anyway – **even though** I feel really tired/stiff/down/ fed-up/anxious'*.

Or if you feel you can't do it that day or at the planned time, think about what you could do instead.

If you noticed problems with your plan

Choosing realistic targets for change is important. Think back to where you started – were you too ambitious or unrealistic in choosing the target you did? Perhaps something didn't happen as you planned, or someone reacted in an unexpected way? Try to learn from what happened.

Q   **How could you change your approach to help you make a more realistic plan next time if that might help?**

_____

_____

_____

   KEY POINT

The very best way of testing out fears and concerns is to act against them and see what happens. If you have planned something you see as important – something that will move you forward, then try to do it even if you don't fancy it on the day. You may get a pleasant surprise. If you feel physically worse with new or worsening symptoms, then check if it's appropriate to still do what you've planned with your doctor or health adviser.

Planning the next steps

The next step is to plan additional activities to build on your first one.

It's helpful to:

- Plan to build activities over the next weeks.

- Introduce activities slowly in a step-by-step way. Use your phone calendar or diary to plan these.

- It's important to remember not to fill every minute of your day. So, your plan should include gaps, rest and relaxation time where you read a paper, listen to the radio, watch TV or play with pets.

- Choose activities that helpfully improve how you feel. In other words, one's that give you a sense of pleasure, are activities you value/see as important or help you feel close to others.

- Include activities you have cut down on doing or stopped, but which you know helped how you felt in the past. Use the checklist on page 102 to work out which one's you want to do.

- Don't forget to **plan activities across the morning, afternoon and evening**, and also across the week.

- It can be tempting to put off some activities simply because it can feel hard. Choose to do some of your **key essential tasks** each week.

- Remember, if a planned activity is important, it's important to do it even if you don't fancy doing it on the day.

- Write down your plan in detail so that you know exactly what you are going to do this week.

- Look for tools to aid when a disability prevents the completion of your tasks.

It's not helpful to:

- Try to alter too many things all at once.

- Overcommit and push yourself too hard – causing you to feel worse and crash back.

- Choose something that is too hard a target to start with.

- Ignore your age, or symptoms of illness and act as if you were 20 once again. Be realistic.

- Be very negative and think *'It's a waste of time'*. Try to experiment to find out if this unhelpful thinking is actually true.

Write your short and medium-term plans here:

Short term – What might you do over the next week or so? This is your next step that you need to plan.

_____

_____

Medium term – What might you aim towards doing over the next few weeks – the next few steps?

_____

_____

SUMMARY

In this workbook you have learned:

- How low mood and stress cause you to do less.

- How reduced activity and avoidance affects you.

- How to identify things you have cut down, or stopped doing which you used to enjoy.

- Which activities help you feel better and consider how to plan these into your life.

- How to build a helpful routine across your day.

Before you go

What have you learned from this workbook?

_____

_____

What do you want to try next?

_____

_____

 Here are some suggested tasks to practice this approach:

- Use the _Vicious cycle of reduced or avoided activity worksheet_ to identify the impact of reduced or avoided activity on your life. You can download this from www.llttf.com/resources.

- Use the _Checklist_ of reduced/avoided activities to identify things that previously gave you a sense of pleasure, achievement or closeness/connection to others.

- Use what you find to plan to reintroduce one or two activities in the next week that can improve how you feel. Introduce these one at a time, and review your progress as you go.

Worksheets to help you practice

Practice is important to help you master this approach. You can get free access to additional worksheets used in this workbook chapter and the wider book at www.llttf.com/resources

From the current workbook, this includes a blank copy of the *Vicious cycle of reduced/avoided activity* and the *Checklist of reduced/avoided activities*.

Acknowledgements

The cartoon illustrations were produced by Keith Chan, kchan75@hotmail.com. Thank you to Mrs Theresa Kelly and Mrs Sue Wood at Five Areas Ltd for their helpful advice and comments on earlier drafts of this book. Also, to those practitioners and Peer mentors at North West Senior and Disability Services in Oregon, USA who inputted into the initial modifications of these resources to suit an older adult readership.

The term Five Areas® is a registered trademark of Five Areas Resources Ltd. Although we hope you find this book helpful, it's not intended to be a direct substitute for consultative advice with a healthcare professional, nor do we give any assurance about its effectiveness in a particular case. Accordingly, neither we nor the author shall be held liable for any loss or damages arising from its use.

Overcoming Depression and Low Mood in Older Adults

A Five Areas® CBT Approach

Using exercise to improve how you feel

Dr Chris Williams

DOI: 10.4324/9781003347637-11

Do you ever notice this?

Walking upstairs makes me out of breath

I feel really down

I need a stair lift to get upstairs

My whole body feels stiff when I've sat in the chair all day

I can't walk to the local shops anymore

I'm needing regular steroid injections to help my arm move freely

I feel great after doing some gardening

I just sit watching the television

Swimming used to make me feel good

I'm needing a frame to walk

I feel too exhausted to do anything

I'm so unfit!

Is this you?

If so, … this workbook is for you.

In this workbook you will:

- Discover how exercise can improve your mood.

- Learn how to use exercise to reduce feelings of tension and anxiety.

- Discover how exercise can help you feel more physically fit, strong, flexible and stable in your balance.

Why exercise is important as we grow older

Physical activity is important throughout life. It affects how we feel both physically and emotionally. As we age, problems like pain due to arthritis, heart or lung problems or illnesses such as stroke, diabetes or cancer can all affect us physically by contributing to reduced activity. That reduced activity can affect us physically and emotionally.

1 **Physically**: Our bodies need regular movement. Without it our muscles lose strength, and we become less flexible and stiffer. This can affect our balance and lead to an increased risk of falls.

2 **Emotionally**: If we do less, and stay in more, it's likely we won't do as many activities that lift our mood. We may also see less of the people we like and are close to. Our mood can drop as a result. You're probably also aware that exercise can have a direct impact on your energy, focus and enthusiasm. Think back to times of life when you've exercised recently or in the past. Did you notice it that physical activity lifted your mood? Many people do.

Exercise also has a direct impact in helping you sleep better and reduces bodily inflammation. This can have a positive impact on how we feel physically and emotionally. It is because of this that there is general advice to exercise and move regularly throughout life – including when we are older.

Health service advice is that we should:

- Increase activity – by moving faster so your heart rate and breathing speed up.

- Build and maintain your bodily strength – for example by using weights.

- There are added benefits of building your core strength and **balance**.

Physiotherapists and other exercise specialists can advise on how best to build these into your day, in a way that is suited to you.

- Exercise can be fun if you choose something that you have previously liked doing. It also comes in many forms. Walking, running, stretching, yoga, pilates, swimming and more.

- It can help you structure and plan your day – rather than just staying in and being inactive.

- It can improve your social life. Exercising with others such as an exercise class, Gym training sessions, tennis, badminton, joining a walking group or going for a swim can help you meet others with a shared interest.

Some things to bear in mind

- If you are physically unwell, you may not be able to do certain exercises for a time or need to reduce the intensity or time you spend on them. Ask your doctor or physical therapist for advice about what you can or can't do if you are ill or have had a recent operation.

- You may have aching muscles to begin with. Make sure you pace things.

- There can be a cost for some activities (e.g. for using a gym or a swimming pool).

KEY POINT

Exercise and injury: Remember it's important to warm up to avoid muscle pulls, aches and strains. Using good techniques and the right equipment, clothing and shoes is also important.

Using the five areas assessment to reflect on your beliefs about exercise

Your thoughts, emotions, thinking, body, behaviour, relationships and life situation can all affect each other.

As we grow older each of the Five Areas® can become caught up in how active we are:

1 **Situations, relationships and practical problems:** When we reduce our activity levels because of age or illness, we can end up feeling isolated and lonely. We might not travel to meet up with people we like. And that can make us feel worse. One opportunity of planning ways of maintaining physical activity is to meet others for example at pilates, yoga or other classes.

2 **Your thinking:** What we think and believe is important as it affects our attitudes to activity. What rules or lessons did we learn about the importance of exercise from seeing key people in our family as they got older? Did key relatives like parents or grandparents continue to be active? Or was our experience that older people stayed indoors, or sat in a chair with a blanket over their knees to keep warm? Did people stay as active as they could, and take the opportunity to use sticks or walking frames or wheelchairs to maintain their mobility if they were needed? Or avoid these even when recommended, as they were seen as embarrassing or unwanted?

Q What are your own reactions to exercise and activity? For example do you see activity as good for you, or a risk if you have heart disease, breathing problems or are struggling with illness? Importantly, for almost all physical conditions, movement is recommended.

_____

_____

3 **Your feelings:** Are you anxious about movement? About getting far from home and feeling worse? About falling? About having other symptoms?

Q Write any fears about exercise here:

_____

_____

4 **Your physical/bodily symptoms and other sensations:** These might include symptoms because of illness. Sensations such as chest pain in angina, dizziness with high or low blood pressure, pain or stiffness in arthritis are common. Symptoms – especially pain and tiredness – can sometimes lead us to over-rest and do less and less. However, over-resting and reduced activity can be bad for us emotionally and physically. The danger is that over time we become stiffer, weaker and frailer.

 ## How do any symptoms/illnesses affect your exercise/activity levels?

_____

_____

5 **Our behaviour/activity levels:** As we grow older, we can lose opportunities to get out. For example if we were working, it's often good for us mentally and physically. Perhaps work gave something to get out of bed for, or we had to walk, get buses or trains or drive to get to and from work. There's also the mental stimulation work offers. With retirement comes an added challenge of how to maintain confidence in getting out and about and travelling as you get older. That's why so many older adults volunteer, continue to work or find simulation and value through hobbies, interests, education courses or clubs.

 ## How do you maintain mental, and social stimulation – and keep your confidence up?

_____

_____

Good news!

The good news is that exercise can be part of maintaining that ability to keep doing things, by leading to improvements in each of the Five Areas®.

Exercise also has a direct impact in helping us sleep better and reduces bodily inflammation, which can have a positive impact on how we feel. This is summarised in Figure 8.1.

How planned exercise can help you feel better

Experiment

You'll need less than 15 minutes to do this experiment. The aim is to test if even a small amount of exercise affects how you feel overall.

Before you start: Think of a physical activity that you can do. This should be something:

• That is realistic, bearing in mind how you are physically at the moment.

• That can be done in just 5–10 minutes to start with.

• You know is within your capabilities and doesn't overly push you.

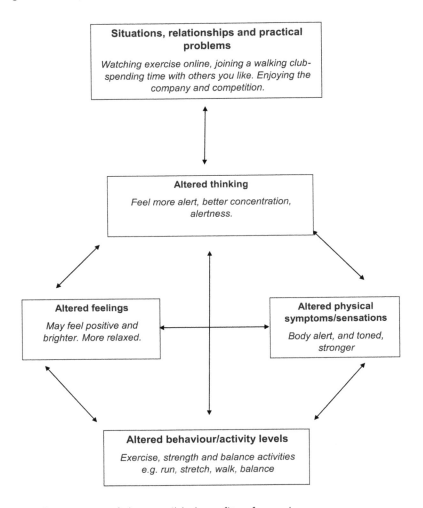

Figure 8.1 A Five Areas® summary of the possible benefits of exercise

Please choose something that doesn't involve vigorous exercise. Here's an example. Walk up and down a flight of stairs three to four times. Take a rest if you get out of breath.

KEY POINT

This isn't asking you to do a workout. You don't need to get changed, work up a sweat or even do warm-up exercises!

Other things you could try are stretching your body, jogging slowly on the spot or walking around the block at a reasonable pace. Remember not to overdo it.

Aim to do something that gets your heart rate up and gets you moving without being excessive. Remember, any benefits can be boosted even more by planning to do activities that are fun or sociable. If you are physically unwell you should always check what is appropriate with your doctor first. Just do what you can.

Each of the Five Areas® is connected. That's why by **increasing your physical activity levels, you can improve how you feel mentally as well as physically**.

Doing your planned exercise

Before you start put a cross on the three lines below to show how you feel right now.

How you feel before your exercise?

Sadness/happiness	Tension/anxiety	Physically in your body
Very sad OK Very happy	Very tense OK Very relaxed	Very tense OK Very relaxed

Now do your 5–10 minutes exercise. Remember, you can stop for a rest if you feel this is too much for you.

Your review

Immediately afterwards please rate your mood again.

How you feel after your exercise?

Sadness/happiness	Tension/anxiety	Physically in your body
Very sad OK Very happy	Very tense OK Very relaxed	Very tense OK Very relaxed

Next: Stop, think and reflect

Have a look at your scores before and after the exercise.

 **Did you notice any changes?**

Write down any changes you noticed:

_____

_____

Overall, do you think you might benefit from planning some exercise in your life as part of your own 'mental fitness' package?

Yes ☐   No ☐   Yes, but… ☐

Yes, but …

There are often lots of things in life that we know are good for us, but we don't do them. Remember, that's just as true in other people's lives as it may be in your own.

Tackling the simple blocks

Often the biggest problems are simple ones:

- Perhaps you just aren't in the habit of doing exercise.

- Or maybe you want to get into the habit of doing exercise but you think it will be too hard. For example it's easy for us to talk ourselves out of it if there's no time.

Many people see exercise as too hard or boring, too expensive, taking too much time – or all of these!

Q What thoughts sometimes block you from doing exercise?

Write them down here:

_____

_____

_____

Planning to do exercise doesn't mean you have to make a big change to your lifestyle. Even **small changes** can make a positive difference. Now find a way to make this easier for yourself, for example fitting it into what you already do each day.

Making a clear plan that works for you

People are often amazed at how empowering and energising it can feel when they get into the habit of exercising as part of their regular daily routine.

- Choose something that gets you going physically.

- Build up the amount of exercise slowly in a gradual and planned way.

- Don't throw yourself into things too quickly (or start too slowly): **pacing is the key**.

- Many people find that doing exercise towards the start of the day helps them to 'get going'. Try to avoid exercising just before going to bed as this can unhelpfully affect your sleep.

- Plan to exercise with a friend or relative. This has the added benefit of encouraging you get started if you find it's difficult. It may also help boost your **sense of closeness**, which again can help your mood.

Planning when and how to exercise

Exercising on a regular basis – even if it is just a short time to begin with – is important. It is often helpful to actively plan this into your day and diary rather than just 'trying to fit it in sometime'. You may find the following **planning task** helpful in making this regular commitment.

My plan to use exercise to help me feel better

What about you? Write your own plan here:

1 **What am I going to do?**

_____

2 **When am I going to do it?**

_____

3 **IS MY PLANNED TASK:**

Useful for understanding or changing how I am?

Yes ☐   No ☐

Clear and specific, so that I will know when I have done it?

Yes ☐   No ☐

Realistic, practical and achievable?

Yes ☐   No ☐

What problems or difficulties could arise – and how could I overcome these?

_____

_____

Now, carry out your plan

Try to do your plan. Good luck!

My review of how it went

Afterwards, even if it went well, stop and reflect on how things went. If things didn't go as you wanted, try to stop, think and reflect so you can learn from this. That way you can put what you're learning into practice so you make better and better plans going forward.

Now write down your own review:

_____

_____

_____

What if symptoms get in the way?

It's quite common to find that you might be tempted to put exercise off *('I'll do it next week')* or talk yourself out of it. Perhaps you might feel worse at the time, perhaps tired, lower in mood, more negative or fed-up? Or it rains or is cold outside.

If that's the case, then choose to change what you say to yourself. Instead of saying *'I was going to do it, but feel really tired/stiff/down/fed up/anxious'*, …

Change it to: ***'I'm going to choose to do it anyway*** *even though I feel really tired/stiff/down/fed-up/anxious'*.

Or if you feel you can't do it that day or at the planned time, think what you could do instead.

KEY POINT

The very best way of testing out fears and concerns is to act against them and see what happens. If you have planned something you see as important – something that will move you forward, don't let feeling bad put you off. You may get a pleasant surprise. If you feel physically worse with new or worsening symptoms, then check if it's appropriate to still do what you've planned with your doctor or health adviser.

SUMMARY

In this workbook you have learned how:

- Exercise can improve your mood.
- You can use exercise to reduce feelings of tension and anxiety.
- Exercise can help you feel more physically fit, strong, flexible and stable in your balance.

Before you go

What have you learned from this workbook?

_____

_____

What do you want to try next?

_____

_____

Here are some suggested tasks to practice this approach:

Try to pick an activity that you want to do, and is realistic for you based on how you feel. Using the plan described earlier, write down in your phone or diary what you will do and when you will do it. And enjoy!

Worksheets to help you practice

Practice is important to help you master this approach. You can get free access to additional worksheets used in this workbook chapter and wider book at www.llttf.com/resources

Acknowledgements

The cartoon illustrations were produced by Keith Chan, kchan75@hotmail.com. Thank you to Mrs Theresa Kelly and Mrs Sue Wood at Five Areas Ltd for their helpful advice and comments on earlier drafts of this book. Also, to those practitioners and Peer mentors at North West Senior and Disability Services in Oregon, USA who inputted into the initial modifications of these resources to suit an older adult readership.

The term Five Areas® is a registered trademark of Five Areas Resources Ltd. Although we hope you find this book helpful, it's not intended to be a direct substitute for consultative advice with a healthcare professional nor do we give any assurance about its effectiveness in a particular case. Accordingly, neither we nor the author shall be held liable for any loss or damages arising from its use.

Overcoming Depression and Low Mood in Older Adults

A Five Areas® CBT Approach

Helpful things you can do

Dr Chris Williams

DOI: 10.4324/9781003347637-12

Do you ever notice this?

Are you doing things that help you, like these?

If not … this workbook is for you.

In this workbook you will:

- Learn about helpful things you can do that can make you feel better.

- Plan some ways to make sure that you do these things, even when you are busy, under pressure or experience physical limitations.

- Consider some next steps to build on this knowledge.

What are helpful activities?

Helpful activities are **helpful because of the effect they have on you and also on others.** Some examples of helpful activities include:

- Talking to, or meeting up with family, friends or neighbours.

- Doing things that improve how you feel, for example getting outside, walking in the park, reading a book or doing yoga – all the things that can fall by the wayside when you begin to struggle.

- Pampering yourself, such as having a special bath with music and candles, or a nice meal, a haircut or something else you enjoy. It doesn't have to be costly.

- Seeking accurate knowledge about how to tackle low mood and depression or cope with physical illness. For example reading books like this one or fact sheets that you can get from organisations that support people living with low mood or chronic illness.

- Seeing your doctor to find out what support is available for you locally. For example whether you should see an expert mental health counsellor or a health or social care practitioner.

- Keeping going – doing the right activities can help overcome low mood. For example get outside and say hello to people you know as you go for a walk. All these things will help you stay confident.

Write down any *helpful* things you have done in the past two weeks:

_____

_____

You may not have thought of this, but it makes sense to also actively plan these things into your week. In this way, you will give yourself little boosts throughout the week.

It can be helpful to create a clear plan to build on these activities over the next days, weeks and months. That way you can build positive changes step by step.

When helpful things can become unhelpful

Sometimes you can think that an activity is helpful, but, in fact, it's part of the problem. For example:

- Drinking a lot to settle your nerves or provide false confidence.

- Avoiding people and events around you that make you feel stressed.

- Seeking reassurance – like an addiction, you keep needing more.

KEY POINT
Many helpful things you do can become unhelpful for you or for others if you rely on them too much or do them all the time.

Now let's move on to possible ways in which you can build more helpful behaviours into your life.

Choosing which helpful activities to build up

You need to identify some helpful activities to plan to work on doing again/more of. The first thing to do is to choose a single helpful activity to work on first.

Look at the following list and check any activity that you used to do, but have cut down or stopped because of how you feel.

Checklist: What helpful things could you plan to start/increase?

Are you:	Check the helpful activities you want to increase/start
Being good to yourself? For example eating regularly and healthily, taking time to enjoy the food.	☐
Doing things for fun/pleasure? For example your hobbies, listening to music, having a nice bath.	☐
Spending time with people you like? For example friends or family.	☐
Seeking support from others whom you trust? Like going to a self-help group (your doctor/health or social care worker can tell you about these groups).	☐
Keeping in touch with others even if you don't feel like it? Pick a level of contact you can cope with, for example by telephone, email or meeting up for coffee.	☐
Stopping, thinking and reflecting on things rather than jumping to conclusions? For example letting upsetting thoughts 'just be' rather than mulling over them.	☐
Finding out accurate information about depression by reading information leaflets, self-help books, etc.?	☐
Pacing yourself – so you don't run out of energy or sit doing very little?	☐

Keeping active physically? For example doing exercise/going for walks/swimming/ gardening/ riding your bike. **Note:** If you had an operation or are physically ill and in pain, you may need to take it easy for a time. But once your doctor says it is okay, try to keep reasonably active. If you rest too much you will find you feel stiffer and more easily tired. Try walking with as relaxed and normal a posture as possible. If you have loss of mobility due to age or impairment, look for alternative ways to get some physical exercise and/or out of your room/house (e.g. chair exercises, mobility scooter for getting out for fresh air and a change of scenery).	☐
Using your sense of humour to cope?	☐
Giving yourself a break/the benefit of the doubt? Remember: No one is perfect.	☐
Taking any prescribed medication regularly and as prescribed? Remember that the medication is there to help.	☐
Using approaches such as relaxation tapes, slow breathing, etc. to deal with tension?	☐
Being honest with trusted others (especially your doctor) about how you really are? If you are struggling, you need to say so, otherwise people will not know, you need help.	☐
Planning time for yourself or you and your partner together? For example you could plan to spend time together talking or going out for a meal, spending time together, watching TV or cuddling?	☐
Anything else you think is helpful for you or others?	

Write in:

_____

Choosing a first target

From your list above, you may have identified several helpful activities you could choose to start or increase. It usually isn't possible to work on multiple areas all at once. You need to decide on **one helpful activity** to with. Pick an activity that can be easily planned into your life.

EXAMPLE: JULIA'S TARGET

Julia has been feeling depressed for a second time in her life. Her children are all grown and have moved away. Julia has found she has felt increasingly ground down by her low mood – and has been doing less and less for herself. She knows that meeting up with others helps her feel better. Julia completes the checklist and decides she will plan some time with her friends.

Now it's your turn

Next, use the checklist on pages 126–7 to choose one helpful behaviour for you to work on first. This is particularly important if you have checked many boxes in the list.

My target: Write down a single helpful behaviour that you want to work on:

_____

 KEY POINT

Ideally this should be a helpful behaviour that has helped you before, but which you have stopped or cut down doing. Choose an activity that you would like to do. You can choose any activity, but it's often helpful to choose things you know from previous experience will help you.

Breaking it down into smaller steps

Some helpful activities can be planned easily. However, some may need more planning. The important thing is to use a **step-by step** approach where no single step seems too large. The first step needs to be something that gets you moving in the right direction.

For some activities, you may need to break down your target helpful behaviour into many smaller steps that you can tackle one at a time. So, to go to the cinema with friends, you might need to decide who to ask, check what films are showing, decide which one to go to, get there and back, etc. You can plan any of these stages using this approach.

Q **Do you need to break your own target helpful behaviour down into something more realistic and achievable?**

Yes ☐ or No ☐

If so, re-write what you want to do:

My updated first step is:

_____

_____

Once you've picked a first step to work on, make a plan to do it.

Make a plan to do it

You need to have a clear plan that states exactly **what** you are going to do and **when** you are going to do it. This will help you to think about what to do and also to predict problems that might arise. Another important part of the plan is to predict what could block the plan.

JULIA'S EXAMPLE

Julia has decided she will plan some time with her friends.

What am I going to do:

I'll contact my friend Sarah and suggest we meet up for lunch in a local coffee shop.

When am I going to do it:

I'll call Sarah this evening at about 8.00 pm – and try to agree a time to meet in the next week.

Is my planned task useful for understanding or changing how I am?

Yes – It will be nice to chat with her, and I know I always like her company.

Clear and specific, so that I will know when I have done it?

Yes – I'll know by 8.30 pm today if I've done it.

Realistic, practical and achievable?

Yes, I have her number. We always used to chat a lot – I've known her since school and we get on well. It would be good to have lunch with her – she's always enjoyed that too.

What problems or difficulties could arise – and how could I overcome these?

I could forget to phone. I could set a phone reminder. Maybe Sarah will be put this evening – if so, I could leave a message with her partner. Maybe she will be busy this week or away? If so, we could plan a meeting another time. If she doesn't answer the phone, I'll send her a text 'hello' and suggest we meet for a coffee.

Julia phones Sarah that evening. The first time she calls the phone is engaged. Julia knows Sarah is in – and phones back a quarter hour later and gets through. Sarah is delighted to hear from her. They chat for ages and arrange to meet for lunch next Tuesday.

What about you? Write your own plan here:

1 What am I going to do?

_____

_____

2 When am I going to do it?

_____

3 Is my planned task:

Q Useful for understanding or changing how I am?

Yes ☐   No ☐

Q Clear and specific, so that I will know when I have done it?

Yes ☐   No ☐

Q Realistic, practical and achievable?

Yes ☐   No ☐

Q What problems or difficulties could arise – and how could I overcome these?

_____

_____

Now, carry out your plan

Put your plan into action.

My Review of how it went

Afterward, even if it went well, stop and reflect on how things went. If things didn't go as you wanted, try to stop, think and reflect so you can learn from this. That way you can put what you're learning into practice so you make better and better plans going forward.

• What went well?

• What didn't go so well?

• How can you take what you've learned so you make better and better plans going forward?

Now write down your own review:

_____

_____

_____

Overcoming Depression and Low Mood in Older Adults: A Five Areas® CBT Approach   © 2024 Five Areas Resources Limited

EXAMPLE: Julia's review

Julia really looks forward to the lunch. On the day this was planned, Sarah phones to say her mother is sick and she can't come. Julia is about to burst into tears, when she thinks, *'Ah well! I didn't think of that!'*. But she then arranges to do the same thing with Sarah on Friday.

That Friday, they have a nice meal and chat. Julia feels a strong sense of happiness, and also a real sense of closeness to her friend. She and Sarah then go for a walk in the park together after lunch. They agree to meet again at Sarah's house next week.

What about you?

If you noticed problems with your plan

Choosing realistic targets for change is important. Think back to where you started – were you too ambitious or unrealistic in choosing the target you did? Perhaps something didn't happen as you planned or someone reacted in an unexpected way? Try to learn from what happened.

> **How could you change your approach to help you make a more realistic plan next time?**

_____

_____

_____

Planning the next steps

Now that you have reviewed how your first step went, the next step is to plan another helpful change to build on this first one.

You can choose to:

- Repeat the same thing you have just completed.

- Move it on a bit more.

- Practice another helpful behaviour from the earlier checklist.

It's helpful to:

- Be realistic. Plan **only** one or two helpful activities over the next week.

- Make sure your **plan** includes breaking down your chosen activity into smaller steps if it doesn't seem realistic and practical to do it all at once.

- Write down your plan in detail so you have a clear idea of what you will do and have predicted things that may block your plan from happening.

It's not helpful to:

- Try to plan too big a change all at once.

- Be negative and think, *'I can't do anything, what's the point, it's a waste of time'.* Experiment to find out if this negative thinking is accurate or helpful.

Write your own short and medium-term plans here:

Short term – What might you do over the next week or so? This is your next step that you need to plan.

_____

_____

Medium term – What might you aim toward doing over the next few weeks – the next few steps?

_____

_____

SUMMARY

In this workbook you have:

- Learned about helpful things you can do that can make you feel better.

- Planned some ways to make sure that you do these things, even when you are busy, under pressure or experience physical limitations.

- Considered some next steps to build on this knowledge.

Before you go

What have you learned from this workbook?

_____

_____

What do you want to try next?

_____

_____

Here are some suggested tasks to practice this approach:

- Use the Checklist of *What helpful things could you plan to start/increase* to identify helpful activities you want to work on.

- Use what you find to plan to reintroduce one or two helpful activities in the next week that can improve how you feel. Introduce these one at a time, and review your progress as you go.

Worksheets to help you practice

Practice is important to help you master this approach. You can get free access to additional worksheets used in this workbook chapter and the wider book at www.llttf.com/resources

Acknowledgements

The cartoon illustrations were produced by Keith Chan, kchan75@hotmail.com. Thank you to Mrs Theresa Kelly and Mrs Sue Wood at Five Areas Ltd for their helpful advice and comments on earlier drafts of this book. Also, to those practitioners and Peer mentors at North West Senior and Disability Services in Oregon, USA who inputted into the initial modifications of these resources to suit an older adult readership.

Overcoming Depression and Low Mood in Older Adults

A Five Areas® CBT Approach

Unhelpful things you do

Dr Chris Williams

DOI: 10.4324/9781003347637-13

Do you ever notice this?

Are you doing things like these?

If so … this workbook is for you.

In this workbook you will:

- Find out about how some activities can make you or others feel worse.

- Learn how to tackle unhelpful behaviours.

- Discover how to make a clear plan to reduce an unhelpful behaviour.

- Consider some next steps to build on this knowledge.

Helpful and unhelpful behaviours

When somebody feels distressed, it is normal to try to do things to feel better. But although their responses may be often helpful, sometimes they can fall into responding unhelpfully. You can find out more about helpful behaviours in the workbook, *Helpful things you can do*.

What are unhelpful behaviours

Some examples of common unhelpful behaviours are:

- Getting angry at others.

- Pushing people away.

- Drinking too much to block how you feel.

- Doing things that go against your values/ideals and how you want to live your life.

- Isolating yourself in your home.

These behaviours are unhelpful because of the effect they have on you and also on others. So, getting angry can end up with you feeling alone, and prevents you getting the help and support the other person would otherwise have offered. So, both you and the other person feel worse as a result. These unhelpful behaviours are one area of the Five Areas® Assessment – *Altered behaviours/activity levels*. What we do (or don't do) can affect each of the other areas of life and worsen how we feel. The aim of this workbook is to help you understand why this pattern happens and also to learn ways of changing that behaviour.

Write down any *unhelpful* things you have done in the past two weeks.

_____

_____

Why do unhelpful behaviours happen?

People tend to do unhelpful things because, often, these actions can make them feel better – **in the short term**. So, an activity like getting drunk might be fun or taking risks might be exciting – for a time. However, they can also backfire and create more problems in the medium and longer term. So eventually, they become part of your problem.

The impact on you of unhelpful behaviours

KEY POINT

Both helpful and unhelpful behaviours make you feel better in the short term. But the key difference between them is that in the longer-term unhelpful behaviours backfire. They can make you or others feel worse. So, they become part of your problem. The good news is that if this applies to you, you can make changes.

Think about any behaviours you do that are unhelpful. Choose just one recent example and write down how it affects you.

What did you do?

Effect on me: Consider the impact on each of the five key areas of your life:

Altered thinking: How did you doing this affect your view of the situation, of you, or of others? Were you living according to your values/ideals? Did it help you see things in helpful, and balanced ways?

_____

_____

Altered feelings/emotions: Did it make you feel happy/content, or ashamed, guilty, low, anxious or irritable?

_____

_____

Altered physical symptoms/bodily sensations: Was what you did good for your body? Or did it make you feel unwell, or put you at risk of longer-term problems like weight gain, an infection, bodily damage or harm?

_____

_____

Altered behaviour: Did it help you develop any helpful habits of responding or keep you stuck in unhelpful or addictive habits of responding?

_____

_____

Q What other negative impacts were there on your life of acting in this way? For example in terms of time spent doing the behaviour/ activity, money spent and in terms of what nicer things you could have done if you were not caught up in acting in this way?

_____

_____

Effect on others: Unhelpful behaviours are often bad both for you and also others.

Q What is the impact of the behaviour on others around you? Was your behaviour helpful or unhelpful for them? Was it a good example to those you care about? Were they upset or shocked in any way? Did you feel embarrassed or want to hide what you were doing from others? Will your behaviour create difficulties with others in the future?

_____

_____

If you have discovered that unhelpful behaviours are part of what's keeping you feeling low or stressed, this means that you have now identified something you can change.

Choosing which unhelpful activities to work on reducing

You need to identify some unhelpful activities to **plan to reduce or stop**. The first thing to do is to choose a single unhelpful activity to work on first.

Look at the following list and check any activity that you are doing and which is having an unhelpful impact on you or others.

As a result of how you feel, are you:	Check the unhelpful activities you want to reduce/stop
Looking to others to make decisions to sort out problems for you?	☐
Losing your temper. Pushing others away by being verbally or physically rude to them? Getting into fights/trouble?	☐
Deliberately harming yourself to block how you feel?	☐
Acting in ways that are against your values/ideals, so you live your life in ways you don't like and make you feel unhappy/guilty?	☐
Taking risks, for example crossing the street without looking or gambling using money you don't have?	☐

(continued)

As a result of how you feel, are you:	Check the unhelpful activities you want to reduce/stop
Checking, cleaning or feel compelled to do things a set number of times or in exactly the 'correct' order so as to make things 'right'? Or spending a lot of time deliberately thinking 'good' thoughts to make things feel 'right' – or counting a set number of times? If so, you should see your doctor, you may have a condition called *obsessive-compulsive disorder*.	☐ ☐
Avoiding having sex with your partner because you are anxious or because you feel unattractive or angry?	☐

Checklist: What unhelpful things could you plan to stop/reduce?

Eating too much to block how you feel ('*comfort eating*') or eating so much that this becomes a 'binge'.	☐
Bingeing with drink, smoking or recreational drugs.	☐
Feeling anxious and aware all the time about symptoms of ill health. If you have this problem, you should discuss with your doctor whether you have symptoms of *health anxiety* or a physical cause of your symptoms.	☐
Making impulsive decisions about important things? For example resigning a volunteer position without really thinking through the consequences.	☐
Setting yourself up to fail.	☐
Trying to spend your way out of how you feel by going shopping ('*retail therapy*').	☐
Becoming very demanding or excessively seeking reassurance from others.	☐
Checking your spouse's health more than is needed.	☐
Anything else you think is unhelpful to you or others?	

Choosing a first target

From your list above, you may have identified several unhelpful activities you could choose to work on reducing or stopping.

It usually isn't possible to work on multiple areas all at once. You need to decide on **one unhelpful activity** to start with. Pick an activity that can be easily planned into your life.

EXAMPLE: **PAUL'S TARGET**

Paul feels down sometimes which makes him want to drink too much. Everything seems hard, and Paul has noticed he quickly loses his temper when he has been drinking. He has been shouting at his partner, Helen. At the time he sees the shouting as letting off steam, but afterwards he feels guilty and even lower in his mood.

Once or twice, Paul has felt like hitting Helen, but instead, he has left the room. Helen is increasingly worried about Paul. His temper outbursts are beginning to make her feel angry at what she sees as unfair criticism. She also feels a little scared. They are drifting apart as a couple as a result, and Paul is spending less time in the house and more in the local bar. Paul completes the checklist and from it decides he wants to work on: *Losing your temper. Pushing others away by being verbally or physically rude to them.*

Do some research

The next thing is to do some research on your unhelpful behaviour. First, record your unhelpful behaviour over several days. Try to work out what it may be that causes you to respond in this way.

Make a written note of:

- When it occurs.

- How much and how often you do it (for example how much you drink, how many times you've sought reassurance, etc.).

- Who you are with and how they act.

- How you feel emotionally at the time – and afterwards.

- What went through your mind at the time – and afterwards.

- Whether you have slept well the night before.

- How you felt emotionally and physically at the time – and afterwards.

- Any other things you tend to do to cope or escape.

- And, anything else that seems to help explain your reaction.

The **purpose** of doing this is to discover more about the issue, and what drives it. It will allow you to work out the different parts of the picture that you might need to tackle in a series of steps.

Each step will need a plan, and needs to be small enough that you can succeed but large enough that you can move forward.

 EXAMPLE

Paul keeps a record of when he gets angry and loses his temper. He realises that several things affect this. It's often when:

- He has slept poorly.

- When his partner Helen wants to tell him in detail about her day.

- When he has been to the bar.

Paul realises there are three separate things here he could work on: (i) to sleep better, (ii) change how he relates to Helen and (iii) tackle how much he drinks at the bar. He reads the *Harmful drinking and you* workbook. He uses this to help him cut down how much he drinks. He finds that changing every other drink to a glass of water or soda really helps.

He then moves on to working through the *Overcoming sleep problems* workbook. He finds this really helps – and he is far less irritable when he has slept better. Finally, Paul returns to this current workbook and decides to focus on how he reacts when Helen wants to tell him in detail about her day. He realises he is responding unhelpfully to her when he gets home. She is wanting to talk and share her life with him – yet he is pushing her away. He decides to use the current workbook to work on that.

Now it's your turn

Look back at your responses and choose **one** behaviour for you to work on first. This is particularly important if you have checked many boxes in the list. It isn't possible to do everything all at once, so you need to decide which **one** area to start with.

My target: Write down a single unhelpful behaviour that you want to change here:

_____

_____

Breaking it down into smaller steps

Some unhelpful activities can be reduced or stopped easily. However, some may need more planning. The important thing is to use a **step-by-step** approach where no single step seems too large. The first step needs to be something that gets you moving in the right direction. For some activities, you may need to break down your target problem behaviour into many smaller steps that you can tackle one at a time. So, to stop drinking you may need to see your doctor for advice, reduce drinking each day of the week, and switch to non-alcoholic drinks some of the time. Later, you might cut our drinking one or two days in the week and build change from there with medical advice as needed. You can plan any of these stages using this approach.

Q Do you need to break your own target unhelpful behaviour down into something more realistic and achievable?

Yes ☐   or   No ☐

_____

_____

_____

If so, re-write what you want to do.

My updated first step is:

_____

_____

Make a plan to do it

You need to have a clear plan that states exactly **what** you are going to do and **when** you are going to do it. This will help you to think what to do and also to predict problems that might arise. Another important part of the plan is to predict what could block the plan.

PAUL'S EXAMPLE

Q What are you going to do?

I need to talk with Helen about how I'm feeling. I want to say that I don't like having all these arguments. That I've been working on that by trying to have less to drink and trying to get some better sleep. That has really helped. Also, I've noticed that I find longer conversations difficult. I need to tell her that when we talk if I look like I'm drifting off it's because of the depression – not because I'm not interested in her. I'm finding it difficult to keep focused on anything much – papers, TV – anything. So, I'm going to suggest to her that I really want to hear what's happening in her life, but can we plan some regular times when we can both sit down together and not feel pressured. Also, can we plan to just chat for say 5 to 10 minutes and no longer.

Q When am I going to do it?

Tomorrow morning, before Helen goes to work. So maybe I could say it over breakfast around 8am.

Q Is my planned task useful for understanding or changing how I am?

Yes – it covers what I want to say.

Q Clear and specific, so that I will know when I have done it?

Yes – I'll know by 8.30am tomorrow if I've done it.

Q Realistic, practical and achievable?

There's a lot to say. I'm pretty sure I'll feel anxious. Maybe I should write it down and give it to her as a letter – or read out the letter to her. I like that idea. I could read it out so I know I've said what I need, and give her the letter to look at again.

Q What problems or difficulties could arise – and how could I overcome these?

We have at least half an hour at that time so it's not too rushed or a time under pressure. I think it should go okay. I could feel anxious, and be tempted to put it off. Or maybe she will be in a rush and not want to listen then. That's unlikely, as I know I'm giving her a lift to work and she doesn't have a first appointment till after 9.15.

Paul goes ahead and writes his letter the evening before. The following morning, Paul passes Helen the letter rather than reading it out. She takes it and reads the letter. She smiles and gives Paul a hug. She tells him she is really happy he's said this. Paul starts to apologise that he meant to read it out to her, but she still looks happy.

What about you? Write your own plan here:

1 **What am I going to do?**

_____

2 **When am I going to do it?**

_____

3 **Is my planned task:**

Q Useful for understanding or changing how I am?

Yes ☐   No ☐

Q Clear and specific, so that I will know when I have done it?

Yes ☐   No ☐

Q Realistic, practical and achievable?

Yes ☐   No ☐

Q What problems or difficulties could arise – and how could I overcome these?

_____

_____

Now, carry out your plan

Put your plan into action.

My review of how it went

Afterward, even if it went well, stop and reflect on how things went. If things didn't go as you wanted, try to stop, think and reflect so you can learn from this. That way you can put what you're learning into practice so you make better and better plans going forward.

- What went well?

- What didn't go so well?

- How can you take what you've learned so you make better and better plans going forward?

Now write down your own review:

_____

_____

EXAMPLE: **PAUL'S REVIEW**

That evening, when Helen gets in, they brew a cup of tea and spend ten minutes talking about Helen's day. Helen then suggests they have a break in the conversation – like he suggested in the letter. They then meet up later for a chat about Paul's day. Both of them feel listened to and are really happy the conversations went well.

What about you?

If you noticed problems with your plan

Choosing realistic targets for change is important. Think back to where you started – were you too ambitious or unrealistic in choosing the target you did? Perhaps something didn't happen as you planned or someone reacted in an unexpected way? Try to learn from what happened.

 How could you change your approach to help you make a more realistic plan next time?

_____

_____

Planning the next steps

Now that you have reviewed how your first step went, the next step is to plan another change to build on this first one.

You can choose to:

- Repeat the same thing you have just completed.

- Move it on a bit more.

- Work on a different unhelpful behaviour from the earlier checklist.

It's helpful to:

- Be realistic. Plan to work on **only** one or two unhelpful activities over the next week.

- Make sure your **plan** includes breaking down your chosen activity into smaller steps if it doesn't seem realistic and practical to do all together.

- Write down your plan in detail so you have a clear idea of what you will do and have predicted things that may block your plan from happening.

It's not helpful to:

- Try to plan too big a change all at once.

- Be negative and think, *'I can't do anything, what's the point, it's a waste of time'*. Experiment to find out if this negative thinking is accurate or helpful.

Write your own short and medium-term plans here:

Short term – What might you do over the next week or so? This is your next step that you need to plan.

_____

_____

_____

Medium term – What might you aim towards doing over the next few weeks – the next few steps?

_____

_____

SUMMARY

In this workbook you have:

- Found out about how some activities can make you or others feel worse.

- Learned how to tackle unhelpful behaviours.

- Discovered how to make a clear plan to reduce an unhelpful behaviour.

- Considered some next steps to build on this knowledge.

Before you go

What have you learned from this workbook?

_____

_____

What do you want to try next?

_____

_____

 Here are some suggested tasks to practice this approach:

- Use the Checklist of *What unhelpful things could you plan to reduce/stop* to identify unhelpful activities you want to work on.

- Use what you find to plan work on one or two unhelpful activities in the next week that can improve how you feel. Focus on these one at a time, and review your progress as you go.

Plan out what to do at a pace that's right for you. Build changes one step at a time. Some problems such as drinking, gambling and others may take lots of time to change direction simply because they can be more addictive. Always seek extra help if you feel stuck.

Some other workbooks you could use

i. Drinking too much or too often

There is a separate workbook called *Harmful drinking*.

 KEY POINT

Be prepared for set-backs and times when you slip back into the problem after a period of improvement. Don't get stuck in self-criticism if that occurs. Instead, pick yourself up, dust yourself off and keep planning. Don't put off asking for help if you are stuck.

ii. Misusing prescribed medication

Sometimes it can be tempting to misuse prescribed antidepressant medication to block how you feel. However, many medicines aren't designed to be used like this, and taking excess unprescribed doses of prescribed medication can cause unwanted side effects or adverse consequences. The separate workbook *Understanding and taking antidepressant medication* can help you with issues like this. Also, speak to your doctor or other prescriber.

iii. Hiding away

Hiding away from others is a form of avoidance. It can occur at times of anxiety, where it's common for people to avoid situations, people or places that scare them. The problem with hiding away is that it makes us feel better in the short term. But like all unhelpful behaviours, it can undermine us in the long term. So, your confidence may reduce, and your world gets smaller. The workbook *Doing things that make you feel better*, addresses how to plan to overcome reduced activity and avoidance, in ways that rebuild your confidence, and help your world get bigger.

iv. Looking to others to make our decisions for us

Looking to others to make decisions on our behalf can mean that over time we lose confidence. There is a section in the workbook *Information for family and friends- how can you offer the best support*, that talks more about this.

Worksheets to help you practice

Practice is important to help you master this approach. You can get free access to additional worksheets used in this workbook chapter and wider book at www.llttf.com/resources

When you need more help

Remember, you are not alone. If you need more help, consider asking:

- People around you, who you know and trust.

- Your doctor or other health or support worker.

- Specialist services and voluntary organisations for help with problems such as addiction, gambling, anger and more. They can be part of your plan.

Acknowledgements

The cartoon illustrations were produced by Keith Chan, kchan75@hotmail.com. Thank you to Mrs Theresa Kelly and Mrs Sue Wood at Five Areas Ltd for their helpful advice and comments on earlier drafts of this book. Also, to those practitioners and Peer mentors at North West Senior and Disability Services in Oregon, USA who inputted into the initial modifications of these resources to suit an older adult readership.

The term Five Areas® is a registered trademark of Five Areas Resources Ltd. Although we hope you find this book helpful, it's not intended to be a direct substitute for consultative advice with a healthcare professional, nor do we give any assurance about its effectiveness in a particular case. Accordingly, neither we nor the author shall be held liable for any loss or damages arising from its use.

PART 4

Noticing and changing unhelpful thinking

Overcoming Depression and Low Mood in Older Adults

A Five Areas® CBT Approach

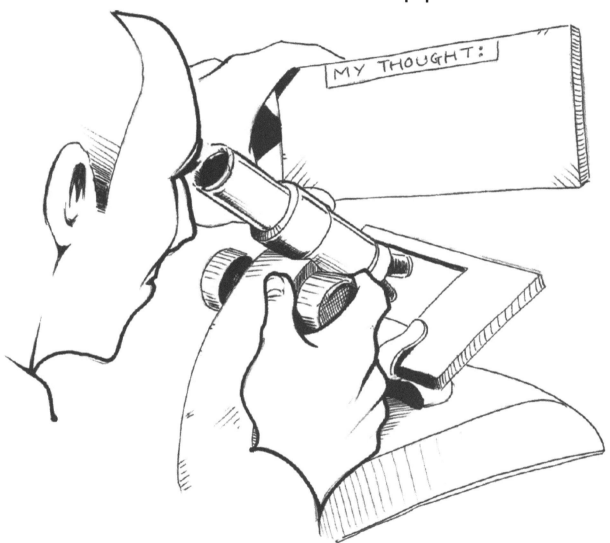

Noticing unhelpful thinking

Dr Chris Williams

DOI: 10.4324/9781003347637-15

Do you ever notice this?

I'm too old to change

I'll never learn how to use the email

I'm a terrible grandmother!

They all think I'm boring

My life is completely useless stuck in the house

I feel so embarrassed feeling like this

I mess everything up

I'm way too old to move somewhere smaller

I can't get her comment out of my mind

I've been so stupid!

I'm a burden on my children

Is this your situation?

If so, ... this workbook is for you.

In this workbook you will learn:

- About seven common unhelpful thinking styles.

- That unhelpful thoughts can worsen how you feel, and unhelpfully alter what you do.

- That you are more prone to slip into unhelpful patterns of thinking at times of low mood or stress. These thoughts are harder to get out of mind at times like this and can make you feel even worse.

- That just noticing and labelling the unhelpful thinking style can make a big difference to how you feel.

A second workbook, *Changing unhelpful thinking* can be used once you feel you have mastered the content of this current workbook.

Introduction

When you feel low or stressed you can:

- Focus on worrying thoughts and fears – these thoughts can make you feel **tense, stressed or panicky**.

- Have unhappy, negative thoughts – these can make you feel **low and sad**.

- Notice frustrated, angry or guilty thoughts about yourself, your situation and about others.

You could also notice **all sorts of upsetting thoughts** about how you feel, your current situation and your future outlook.

Noticing unhelpful thinking

The first step to changing unhelpful thinking is to start noticing how **common** it is in your life.

> **KEY POINT**
>
> Frustration, anger, distress, shame, guilt and feeling down; worsening physical symptoms such as tiredness, pain or stiffness; and altered behaviour such as avoiding people, places and situations are often linked to unhelpful thinking.

Unhelpful thoughts are habits of thinking that make us *feel* worse emotionally or physically, or unhelpfully alter what we *do*. We'll discover more about these unhelpful impacts shortly.

Going through the checklist below will help you to recognise some of the most common unhelpful styles of thinking.

The Unhelpful Thinking Styles Checklist

Unhelpful thinking style	Some typical thoughts	Check here if you have noticed this – even if just sometimes
Being your own worst critic/ bias against yourself.	I judge myself harshly. I overlook my strengths and positive things. I dwell on my failures. I downplay my achievements.	☐
Putting a negative slant on things (negative mental filter).	I see life through dark, tinted glasses. The glass is half empty rather than half full. Whatever I've done it's never enough to give me a sense of achievement. I tend to focus on the bad side of every situation.	☐
Having a gloomy view of the future (make negative predictions).	I predict things will stay bad or just get worse. I always expect to fail.	☐
Jumping to the very worst conclusion (catastrophising).	I tend to predict that the very worst will happen.	☐
Having a negative view about how others see you (mind-reading).	I often think that others don't like me or think badly of me without any reason for it.	☐
Unfairly taking responsibility for things.	I feel guilty about things even if they aren't really my fault.	☐
Making extreme statements or rules.	I use the words *'always'* and *'never'* a lot. If one bad thing happens to me, I often say *'just typical'* because it seems this always happens. I make myself a lot of *'must'*, *'should'* *'ought'* or *'got to'* rules.	☐

Almost everyone experiences these sorts of thoughts each and every day. This doesn't mean that:

- You think like this **all** the time.
- You have to experience **all** of the unhelpful thinking styles.

Where do unhelpful thoughts come from?

While growing up, people learn to relate to others from their parents, teachers and friends. We're also influenced by other things such as TV, magazines and social media. These can often portray a picture of perfection that is impossible for anyone to live up to in the real world. Many people mentally beat themselves up over things they *must/should/ought* to do, or over things they think they haven't done well. In doing so, they often overlook that actually they are doing a far better job than they are giving themself credit for.

How does unhelpful thinking affect you?

Often people believe unhelpful thoughts just because they 'feel' true. This is because of how you're feeling in yourself. And you can forget to check out how true these thoughts really are.

Usually when you notice these kinds of thoughts you may feel a little upset, but then quickly move on and carry on with life. But there are times when you may be more prone to these thoughts and find them harder to dismiss. For example when you have a problem you're finding hard to cope with or if you're distressed and worn down. At times like this, you may also dwell on such thoughts more than usual and then find it harder to move on from them.

Remember that what you think can have a powerful effect on how you feel and what you do. So unhelpful thinking can lead to:

1 **Mood changes** – you may become down and upset, anxious/stressed, guilty, ashamed or angry.

2 **Behaviour changes** – you may reduce or stop doing things, or avoid doing activities that seem too much. Or, you end up reacting in ways that backfire, such as pushing others away, drinking too much or isolating yourself.

3 **Physical changes in our body:** Unhelpful thoughts can lead to a focus on symptoms such as tiredness and pain, increased tension or stiffness or physical agitation so you find it hard to settle or sleep. They may also contribute to symptoms directly as a result of mental tension such as noticing head, chest, bodily or tummy pains, a rapid heart, faster breathing or feeling hot, sweaty or clammy.

 KEY POINT

Thinking in these unhelpful ways means that you're only looking at part of the picture. Because of this, these thinking styles are often not true.

 EXAMPLE: WALKING DOWN THE STREET.

Situation: You are walking down the road and someone you know walks past and says nothing. They don't smile or meet your eye – they just walk by.

Unhelpful thought: *'They doesn't like me'.* This is an unhelpful thinking style: *mind-reading* (that the person doesn't like you); jumping to the worst conclusion; being your own worst critic; being biased against your own self.

Altered feelings: Low/down and upset; anxious about your friendship. Perhaps angry or irritated at how rude they have been.

Altered bodily sensations: Tense, heart speeds up, sick feeling in your stomach. Lose energy and feel exhausted.

Altered behaviour: Perhaps you feel so low and exhausted you turn around and go home. In the longer term, you avoid meeting up with that person to avoid upset.

Stop, think and reflect: *'You never checked out if this was the real reason. Maybe they just didn't see you or were distracted by a worry in their own life?'*

But what if my unhelpful thoughts are true?

At times when we are stressed or low, we tend to jump to conclusions and accept the worst about ourselves, our situation and the future. Often these thoughts are both unhelpful and also untrue. That doesn't mean we never get things wrong, or every single person we know likes us all the time, etc.

Sometimes when we mind-read we may be right – someone we know doesn't like us and judges us badly. But remember that when you feel low you tend to worry too much about these things – and think that almost **everyone** thinks this way without any reason for it to be true.

The good news is that it's possible to help change things to get back into a more balanced and helpful way of seeing things.

Noticing extreme and unhelpful thinking

The first step to changing unhelpful thinking patterns is to practice **spotting** when they happen. You may find there are a number of unhelpful thinking styles that you fall into again and again. Once you notice these patterns of thinking, you can step back and choose to respond differently.

Here are some examples of how extreme thinking can affect how you feel and what you do.

EXAMPLE: SALLY'S UNHELPFUL THINKING (1)

Sally is feeling low and has started to avoid meeting people because of reduced confidence. One day, a friend phones inviting Sally and her partner to lunch at the weekend. Sally says she and her partner John will come. On the day she sits at one end of the table and avoids speaking. She mind-reads that '*Everyone else thinks I'm boring*' and she feels stressed and anxious, causing her to withdraw even more into herself. Sally is also annoyed because John seems to be enjoying himself. She thinks, '*He's more interested in them than me – he doesn't care.*' She is physically tense – with a rapid heart and breathing.

After the main course, Sally tells John that she is feeling unwell and needs to be taken home. She gets up and goes to sit in the car, not saying goodbye to most of the group.

Sally's avoidance and mind-reading prevent her discovering that she would have really enjoyed things if she had started talking to others. Instead, she sat alone at the end of the table, cut off from the rest of them.

Afterwards she is left '*feeling silly*' for not having talked more to the others – and also angry at John. John is also annoyed with her. He was enjoying the gathering, and thinks that Sally has been rude for not saying goodbye to everyone. He feels frustrated and criticises her. They both go to sleep that night angry at the other. Sally's experiences are summarised in Figure 11.1.

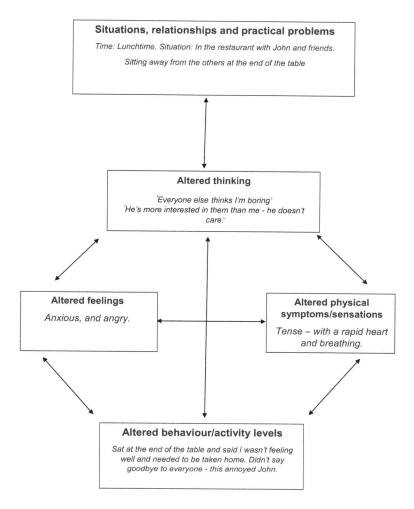

Figure 11.1 Sally's Five Areas® Thought Review of this time when she felt worse

Completing your own Thought Review

Now let's look in detail at a specific time when **you** felt worse.

First, try to think yourself back into a situation in the past few days when you felt worse emotionally or physically. To begin with **don't choose a time when you have felt very much worse**. Instead, pick an occasion when you were just a **bit** upset – for example noticing some tension, or symptoms, anger or guilt. Try to slow it down as you think back through the situation so that you're as accurate as you can be.

TASK: Complete a Thought Review of a time when you felt worse.

Once you have chosen a time when you felt slightly worse, *stop, think and reflect* as you go through the five different areas that can be affected.

Use the blank Five Areas® Thought Review in Figure 11.2 to go through what you noticed in each of the Five Areas®

Download: You can download additional blank Thought Review sheets from www.llttf.com/resources

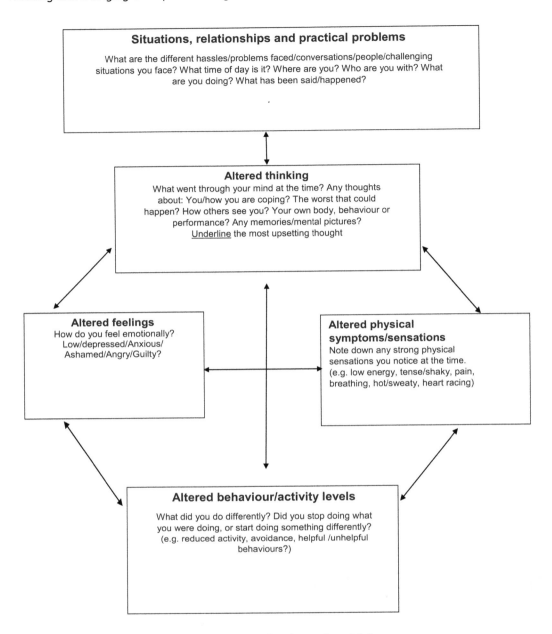

Figure 11.2 My own Five Areas® Thought Review of a time when I felt worse

The Five Area® approach shows that **what you think** about a situation or problem may **affect how you feel** physically and emotionally. It also may alter **what you do** (altered behaviour).

Q **Does your Thought Review help you understand more about what happened at that time you felt worse?**

Yes ☐   No ☐

The best way of becoming aware of your thinking is to try to notice the times when your mood unhelpfully alters (for example at times when you feel upset) or when you feel physically worse. When you notice that change ask *'What's going through my mind right now?'*

We all have all kinds of thoughts during the day. The thoughts we need to spot and then change are those that worsen how we feel and/or affect what we do.

Using the Thought Review worksheet

- Practice using the approach whenever you notice your mood, bodily sensations or behaviour are changing unhelpfully. In this way, you'll find it easier to notice and change your extreme and unhelpful thinking.

- Try to notice your unhelpful thoughts **as soon as possible** after you notice your mood or body change.

- If you can't do this immediately, try to think yourself back into the situation so that you are as clear as possible in your answers later on when you do this task.

SUMMARY

In this workbook you have learned:

- About seven common unhelpful thinking styles.

- That unhelpful thoughts can worsen how you feel, and unhelpfully alter what you do.

- That you are more prone to slip into unhelpful patterns of thinking at times of low mood or stress. These thoughts are harder to get out of mind at times like this and can make you feel even worse.

- That just noticing and labelling the unhelpful thinking style can make a big difference to how you feel.

Before you go

What have you learned from this workbook?

_____

_____

What do you want to try next?

_____

_____

It's important you get skilled at spotting your own unhelpful thinking styles. Try to do this several times a day and use the *Thought Review* worksheet to help you with the task.

Here are some suggested tasks to practice this approach:

- Use the Thought Review worksheet to carry out a thought investigation on **four** occasions when your mood unhelpfully altered.

- **Stop and think** which unhelpful thinking style(s) you noticed during these times and **reflect** on the helpfulness of the thoughts on how you feel and what you do.

- To begin to ask yourself, *'are the thoughts actually **true**?'* How could I see things more helpfully and accurately?

Suggested reading

Once you feel you are able to spot your own unhelpful thinking, then the next workbook to read is *Changing extreme and unhelpful thinking*.

Worksheets to help you practice

Practice is important to help you master this approach. You can get free access to additional worksheets used in this workbook chapter and the wider book at www.llttf.com/resources

Acknowledgements

The cartoon illustrations were produced by Keith Chan, kchan75@hotmail.com. Thank you to Mrs Theresa Kelly and Mrs Sue Wood at Five Areas Ltd for their helpful advice and comments on earlier drafts of this book. Also, to those practitioners and Peer mentors at North West Senior and Disability Services in Oregon, USA who inputted into the initial modifications of these resources to suit an older adult readership.

The term Five Areas® is a registered trademark of Five Areas Resources Ltd. Although we hope you find this book helpful, it's not intended to be a direct substitute for consultative advice with a healthcare professional, nor do we give any assurance about its effectiveness in a particular case. Accordingly, neither we nor the author shall be held liable for any loss or damages arising from its use.

Overcoming Depression and Low Mood in Older Adults

A Five Areas® CBT Approach

Changing unhelpful thinking

Dr Chris Williams

DOI: 10.4324/9781003347637-16

Do you ever notice this?

I'm too old to change

I'll never learn how to use the email

I'm a terrible grandmother!

They all think I'm boring

My life is completely useless stuck in the house

I feel so embarrassed feeling like this

I mess everything up

I'm way too old to move somewhere smaller

I can't get her comment out of my mind

I've been so stupid!

I'm a burden on my children

Is this you?

If so, ... this workbook is for you.

Introduction

This is the second of two workbooks that looks at the area of unhelpfully altered thinking.

In this workbook you will:

• Briefly review how your Thought Review practice went.

• Use a *Thought Change Approach* to practice responding differently to unhelpful thoughts.

Since reading the previous workbook

In the first workbook addressing unhelpful thinking – *Noticing unhelpful thinking* it was suggested you try and complete several tasks. Have you been able to do each of these?

They were to:

• Use the *Thought Review Worksheet* to carry out a thought review on four occasions when your mood unhelpfully altered

   Yes ☐   No ☐

• **Stop and think** which unhelpful thinking style(s) you noticed during these times – and to **reflect** on the helpfulness of the thoughts on how you feel and what you do.

   Yes ☐   No ☐

• To begin to ask yourself, *'are the thoughts actually* **true***?'* How could I see things more helpfully and accurately?

   Yes ☐   No ☐

This current workbook will build on this work, and the previous workbook to help you begin to learn new skills to respond differently to the unhelpful thoughts that can keep you feeling worse.

Revision: Noticing unhelpful thoughts

You have already practiced identifying unhelpful thoughts in the *Noticing unhelpful thinking* workbook.

In that workbook you learned to:

1 Watch for times when you feel worse emotionally (for example time when you felt low or anxious), or became aware of changes in your body (such as feeling tired or physically unwell), or when you noticed an unhelpful change in your behaviour (such as avoidance or reduced activity). Then try to notice what is going through your mind at that time. You were then asked to underline the most upsetting thought.

2 Use the Thought Review approach to carry out a Five Areas® Assessment of the changes you noticed at the time.

Thoughts that are **unhelpful** are the target for change in these workbooks. These are the sort of thoughts that unhelpfully affect how you feel and alter what you do.

How not to respond to upsetting thoughts

Sometimes people try to cope with low mood by **trying not to think about it**. Is this an effective strategy? In order to test out how effective it is, try this practical experiment.

TASK: Please try very hard for the next 30 seconds not to think about a white polar bear.

After you have done this, think about what happened. Was it easy not to think about the white polar bear or did it take a lot of effort?

You may have noticed that trying hard not to think about it actually made it worse and brought thoughts or images of a white polar bear into your mind even more.

Alternatively, you may have spent a lot of mental effort trying hard to think about something else such as a blue polar bear, or something completely different instead such as a car.

Conclusion

Trying not to think about something can sometimes cause the thought to become even more intrusive and troubling. For many people, trying hard to ignore their worries and not think about them is therefore usually not very effective and may actually worsen the problem. Instead, you can learn new ways of responding to unhelpful thoughts.

Examples of extreme and unhelpful thoughts include:

  i Judgmental comments about ourselves – for example:

  - *'I'm really bad at doing that'.*

  - *'I messed that up'.*

  ii A negative view about what is going on – for example:

  - *'It's been a terrible week'.*

  - *'Just typical - things **always** go wrong'.*

  iii A negative view of the future – for example:

  - *'I'll never get better'.*

  - *'It's all downhill from here'.*

If anyone thought, believed and dwelled on upsetting thoughts like these, it would tend to make them worse. It might also cause them to cut down on doing things, so they stay in rather than go out, and isolate themselves rather than seeing friends and family.

KEY POINT

Often someone who is depressed or anxious believes their unhelpful thoughts and doesn't question their accuracy. This is important because many upsetting thoughts are extreme and inaccurate as well as unhelpful.

Changing unhelpful thinking

The following skills aim to help you to begin to question the stream of unhelpful thoughts that pop', into mind through the day when you feel low or anxious.

Pick a single unhelpful thought

It is best at first to choose an unhelpful thought about something that has happened or that has been said. Something that made you feel worse or caused you to react in ways that worsened the situation.

- Choose **just one thought** to question at a time.

- Clearly identify and write down what the thought is. If you completed a Thought Review – perhaps choose a thought that you underlined as having an impact on you.

Write it here:

_____

_____

At the time you felt worse:

Rate how much you believed the thought

Rate how much the thought worsened how you felt emotionally

Rate the impact it had on your behaviour/activity level

Reducing the unhelpful impact of the thought

The following five steps can help reduce the impact of unhelpful thoughts. You can use as many or as few of the following steps as you need.

1 Label the thought as *'just one of those unhelpful thoughts'*, rather than *'the truth'*.

2 Stop, think and reflect – and don't get caught up in the thought.

3 Experiment. Act against it. Don't be put off from what you were going to do.

4 Respond by giving yourself a truly caring and kind response.

5 Put the thought in the dock and imagine you're a judge or jury and consider the evidence in a logical way. Unhelpful thoughts aren't always accurate.

Let's look at each of the steps one at a time and try the approach out with your own thought.

Step 1: Label the thought as 'just one of those unhelpful thoughts' rather than the truth

Look at the thought you are going to work on. Which of the unhelpful thinking styles does it show?

The unhelpful thinking styles checklist

Unhelpful thinking style	Some typical thoughts	Check here if you have noticed this – even if just sometimes
Being your own worst critic/ bias against yourself.	I judge myself harshly. I overlook my strengths and positive things. I dwell on my failures. I downplay my achievements. I focus on what's physically wrong with me.	☐
Putting a negative slant on things (negative mental filter).	I see life through dark, tinted glasses. The glass is half empty rather than half full. Whatever I've done it's never enough to give me a sense of achievement.	☐
Having a gloomy view of the future (make negative predictions).	I predict things will stay bad or just get worse. I always expect to fail.	☐
Jumping to the very worst conclusion (catastrophising).	I tend to predict that the very worst will happen.	☐
Having a negative view about how others see you (mind-reading).	I often think that others don't like me because of my disability or think badly of me without any reason for it.	☐
Unfairly taking responsibility for things.	I feel guilty about things even if they aren't really my fault. I think I'm responsible for everyone and everything.	☐
Making extreme statements or rules.	I use the words '*always*' and '*never*' a lot. If one bad thing happens to me, I often say '*just typical*' because it seems this always happens. I make myself a lot of '*must*', '*should*' '*ought*' or '*got to*' rules.	☐

KEY POINT

If the thought doesn't show one of the unhelpful thinking styles then you should stop here. Choose another time when you feel more depressed, upset, worried, guilty, panicky, or angry or notice bodily changes such as feeling more tired or physically unwell, or a behaviour change such as avoidance or reduced activity. Then complete Step 1 again until you identify a thought that is an unhelpful thinking style. That sort of thought is a good target for change. Then move on to Step 2.

Step 2: Stop, think and reflect – don't get caught up in it

Simply noticing the unhelpful thought can be a powerful way of getting rid of it.

- **Label** the upsetting thought as **just another** of those unhelpful thoughts. These are just a part of what happens when you're upset. It's part of distress – it's not the true picture. You could say to the thought: *'I've found you out – I'm not going to play that game again!'*

- Allow the thought to **just be**. Don't get caught up in it. Like a celebrity, such thoughts love attention. They're just not worth it. Take a mental step back from the thought as if observing it from a distance. You can choose to move your attention to other more helpful things for example future plans, or recent things you have done well or even better on to the task or conversation in hand. Really engage in what you are doing so that task or person is the focus of your attention. Don't be distracted and knocked off course by the unhelpful thought.

Q **Reflect again- how does the thought look now?**

_____

_____

_____

Step 3: Experiment – act against it. Don't be put off from what you were going to do

Unhelpful thinking unhelpfully alters what you do. The thought may try to push you to:

- *Stop, reduce or avoid d*oing something you planned to do. This leads to a loss of pleasure and achievement, or you may avoid other people and social situations, and become more isolated. In the longer term, these changes can restrict your life and undermine your confidence.

- *Respond unhelpfully* like drinking too much alcohol to cope or by pushing others away. This ends up backfiring and worsening how you or others feel.

Make an **active choice** to act against the thought and choose to live by your values/the things that really matter to you.

EXPERIMENT:

Choose not to be bullied by the thought into unhelpfully changing what you do. Choose to react helpfully rather than unhelpfully. If the thought is saying to do something unhelpful, do the opposite and see what happens. So, if an extreme and unhelpful thought says *don't do* something – for example don't go to a friend's birthday party – then do it and test out whether you enjoy it. So, if a thought says you won't enjoy going to that party, go and test out if you do.

To stand up to the bully, it's helpful to:

- **Keep doing** what you planned to do anyway. Stay active.

- **Face your fears**. Act against unhelpful thoughts that tell you that everyday things are too scary and you should avoid them.

It's unhelpful to:

- Get pushed into not doing everyday things by the thoughts.

- Let fear rule your life.

- Block how you feel with drink or street drugs, misusing prescribed medication or by seeking reassurance.

- Respond in ways that act against your values/ideals of how you want to live.

 EXAMPLE: SALLY'S EXPERIMENT

Sally finds herself mind-reading her friends at aqua aerobics. Since she began wearing a colostomy bag, she worries that it will leak in the pool and that her friends share this belief. Though her doctor has assured her this will not happen, Sally has not returned to the pool for several weeks. Sally knows it is very important for her to exercise. Her friends continue to ask when she will return to class. Sally decided to ask her friend Lisa if her swimming with a colostomy bag bothers her. Lisa assures her it does not, so Sally decides to go with her to the next class.

Going to the class helps Sally change her thoughts and feel less anxious.

By choosing to go to the class, enjoying it and talk to others, Sally realises some important things:

- First, people were friendly.

- Second, she did enjoy the class – especially when she chatted to Lisa.

Write your own experiment here:

_____

_____

Decide **what** you will do and **when** you will do it. You can make a note in your phone diary or calendar to help remind you to do it.

Step 4: Respond by giving yourself a truly caring and kind response

When someone feels low, they often can say things to themselves that they would never say to someone they care about. And they say it in an angry, dismissive and nasty tone. If a friend was troubled by a thought or worry, you would offer words of advice to soothe and encourage them. You would be kind and compassionate to them. How can you say similar kind and encouraging things to yourself?

EXAMPLE: SALLY'S KIND THOUGHTS

Sally thinks back to what her mother would have said. These are words of support and love: *'You know we all love you Sally. People often lose their confidence when they feel upset. Don't worry that you didn't chat much with your friends at the pool this time – you did well getting out in the first place, it's not worth upsetting yourself about. You can always chat with Lisa more next time.*

Q What would someone who wholly and totally loved you say to you? Imagine you have the best friend in the world. Someone who is on your side, totally loving and caring. What words of kind encouragement would they say to you? You might choose a close friend or relative, or perhaps a famous person from literature, or, if you have a religious faith, examples from your scriptures. Whoever you choose, you need to be aware that the response will be unconditionally positive, caring and supportive.

Write their caring advice here:

_____

_____

_____

Once you have written it down, try to also speak it out loud (when you're alone!) – and say the words to yourself again and again in a compassionate voice.

Reflect on this – choose to apply their words in your own situation. Trust and believe what they say.

Step 5: Put the thought in the dock and challenge it.

Our upsetting thoughts are often incorrect and untrue. Imagine you're a judge or jury and consider the evidence in a logical way.

Ask yourself the seven thought challenge questions. Complete the following table below to help you work through this process.

The seven thought challenge questions	Your response
1. What would you tell a friend who said the same thing?	
2. Are you basing this on how you feel rather than on the facts?	
3. What would other people say? Would they be more encouraging?	
4. Are you looking at the whole picture? What are you overlooking?	

(continued)

The seven thought challenge questions	Your response
5. Does it really matter so much?	
6. What would I say about this looking back on this in six weeks or six months?	
7. Do I apply one set of standards to myself and another to others? Am I being harder on myself than on others?	

Once you've done this, re-review the impact of your thought now. Does it seem as powerful or upsetting?

How much do you believe the unhelpful thought: Improved ☐   Same ☐   Worse ☐

The impact on your feelings: Improved ☐   Same ☐   Worse ☐

The impact on your behaviour/activity: Improved ☐   Same ☐   Worse ☐

Stop, think and reflect: Is this different from how you felt at the time? Has your view changed during the thought change process? If so, which of the five steps helped the most?

_____

_____

_____

Taking what works for you

When you use the approaches described above in this workbook, you'll probably find that some of the steps work better for you than some others. Build on the ones that work for you into your own reaction when you notice upsetting thoughts.

Discussing your thoughts, fears and concerns with others can sometimes help you get them into a different perspective.

SUMMARY

In this workbook you have learned to:

- Review how your thought review practice went.

- Use an approach to respond differently to unhelpful thoughts.

- Practiced the *Thought Change Approach* to help manage your unhelpful thoughts.

Before you go

What have you learned from this workbook?

_____

_____

What do you want to try next?

_____

 Here are some suggested tasks to practice this approach.

- Use the _Thought Review_ worksheet to carry out a thought investigation some further occasions when your mood unhelpfully altered.

- Stop and think which unhelpful thinking style(s) you noticed during these times and reflect on the helpfulness of the unhelpful thoughts on how you feel and what you do.

- Use the _Thought Change worksheets_ to ask yourself, are the thoughts actually true? How could I see things more helpfully and accurately?

An additional blank copy of the two worksheets is included at the end of this workbook.

Worksheets to help you practice

Practice is important to help you master this approach. A blank _Thought Review_ sheet is included at the end of the chapter (Figure 12.1). This is followed by a simple prompt sheet summarising the different steps of the Thought Change process (Figure 12.2). You can get free access to additional worksheets used in this workbook chapter and the wider book at www.llttf. com/resources

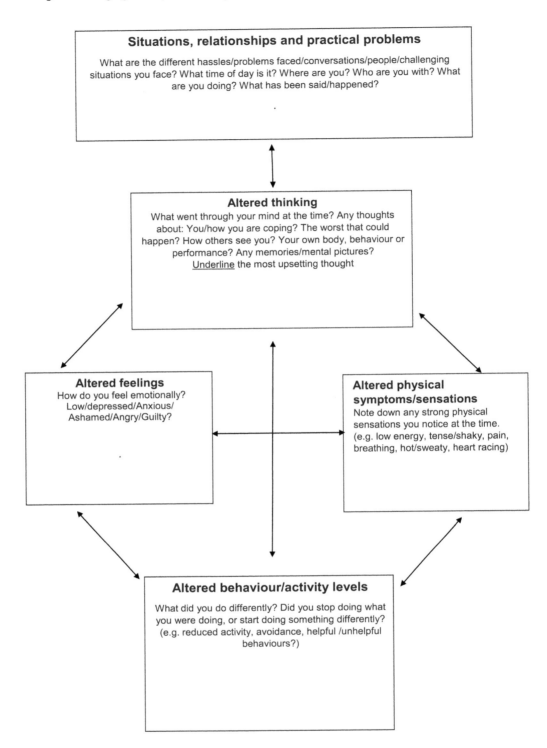

Figure 12.1 My own Five Areas® Thought Review of a time when I felt worse

---

1.   **Label the thought as 'just one of those unhelpful thoughts'.**
- Am I being my own worst critic? (Bias against yourself)
- Am I focusing on the bad in situations? (A negative mental filter)
- Am I making negative predictions about the future? (A gloomy view of the future)
- Am I jumping to the very worst conclusion? (Catastrophising)
- Am I second-guessing that others see me badly without actually checking if it's actually true? (Mind-reading)
- Am I taking unfair responsibility for things that aren't really my fault/taking all the blame?
- Am I using unhelpful must/should/ought/got to statements? (Making extreme statements or setting impossible standards).

---

2. Stop, think and reflect: Don't get caught up in the thought.

Just let the thought be.

3. Experiment and act against it:
- Don't be put off from what you were going to do.
- Keep active. Face your fears.
- Keep to your plan. Respond helpfully.
- Don't be bullied. Act against the unhelpful thought and see what happens.

Task: What things could you do to experiment to undermine and act against the extreme and unhelpful thought?

4. Respond by giving yourself a truly kind and caring response - for example what would someone who loved you wholly and totally say? Speak it out loud if you can.

Write their kind words here:

5. Put the thought in the dock and ask yourself the 7 thought challenge questions:

What would I tell a friend that said the same thing?

Am I basing this on how I feel rather than the facts?

What would other people say?

Am I looking at the whole picture?

Does it really matter so much?

What would I say looking back 6 weeks or six months from the future?

Do I apply one set of standards to myself and another to others?

Based on your answers above how do you now view the unhelpful thought?:

	Improved	Same	Worse
How much do you believe the unhelpful thought:	☐	☐	☐
The impact on your feelings:	☐	☐	☐
The impact on your behaviour/activity:	☐	☐	☐

Figure 12.2 My Thought Change worksheet

Acknowledgements

The cartoon illustrations were produced by Keith Chan, kchan75@hotmail.com. Thank you to Mrs Theresa Kelly and Mrs Sue Wood at Five Areas Ltd for their helpful advice and comments on earlier drafts of this book. Also, to those practitioners and Peer mentors at North West Senior and Disability Services in Oregon, USA who inputted into the initial modifications of these resources to suit an older adult readership.

The term Five Areas® is a registered trademark of Five Areas Resources Ltd. Although we hope you find this book helpful, it's not intended to be a direct substitute for consultative advice with a healthcare professional, nor do we give any assurance about its effectiveness in a particular case. Accordingly, neither we nor the author shall be held liable for any loss or damages arising from its use.

PART 5

Improving sleep, tackling alcohol misuse, understanding and using antidepressant medication

Overcoming Depression and Low Mood in Older Adults

A Five Areas® CBT Approach

Overcoming sleep problems

Dr Chris Williams

DOI: 10.4324/9781003347637-18

Do you ever notice this?

Is this you?

If so, … this workbook is for you.

In this workbook you will:

- Learn about sleep and sleeplessness, and the normal changes in sleeping that occur as we grow older.

- Discover some common causes of sleep problems.

- Understand more about the pitfalls of taking sleeping tablets.

- Learn how to record your sleep pattern and identify things that can worsen your sleep.

- Discover changes that can help you sleep better.

What is enough sleep?

How much sleep you need depends on the person. Some people function well after sleeping only four to six hours a day, whereas others need as many as 10 or 12 hours a day. Both extremes are quite normal. The amount we sleep changes over the lifetime with babies sleeping much of the day and older adults often needing less sleep than earlier in adult life. So, you might notice you are sleeping less than before without feeling more tired than usual.

What causes sleeplessness?

Most people have problems sleeping from time to time. Sleep problems often start after an upsetting life event or they can be a result of your lifestyle. Many psychological problems can also upset sleep. These include anxiety, depression, anger, guilt, shame and stress. Physical problems such as back and neck pain, restless legs, heart failure, breathlessness and sleep apnoea can also stop you sleeping.

A Five Areas® Assessment of sleeplessness

This section helps you think about how poor sleep can affect each of the Five Areas® of your life.

Area 1: Situations, relationships and practical problems

A Problems caused by the people and events around us

   One of the most common causes of sleeplessness is our reaction to things going on around us. External pressures like problems in relationships, arguments, looking after a poorly partner, friend, child or grandchild, worries about bills and more can become a focus.

Q Am I unable to sleep because of things going on with people and events in my life?

Yes ☐   No ☐   Sometimes ☐

If you answered *'Yes'* or *'Sometimes'*, these could be targets for change when you think about how to build on this session later.

KEY POINT

A key decision is whether to approach the difficulty as a practical problem (needing the *Practical Problem solving* workbook), a relationship needing to be rebalanced (needing the *Being assertive* or the *Building relationships with your family and friends* workbooks) or is to do with changing altered thinking (see Area 2 below).

B   Problems with your bed and bedroom

Problems with noise

- Noises that vary or come out of the blue can often wake us. For example if you have noisy neighbours, could you ask them to turn down their television or music? Have you thought about fitting double glazing or secondary glazing inside windows to reduce noise? Or use earplugs? This needn't be expensive and many reasonably priced options are available.

- Or perhaps your partner snores? Are there solutions for them including anti-snoring mouth guards, them losing weight, using earplugs, or them or you moving to another room?

A poor mattress

- Is your bed comfortable?

- If your mattress is quite old, can you turn it over, rotate it or perhaps even change it? You may be able to add extra support, such as a board or old door underneath it.

You find it too hot/cold

- What about the temperature of the room where you sleep? If the room is either very cold or very hot this might make it hard to go to sleep.

- If your bedroom is too hot, try opening a window or using a fan. If it's too cold, think about wrapping up with an extra blanket or using a heated underblanket. Or, you could think about insulation, draught excluders, or double-glazing, turning up the heat, or using a hot water bottle or cherrystone microwavable pillow for warmth* or to cool you down.

Problems with excessive light

- Is there too much light in the room? If bright lights such as streetlights come through your curtains, this can also prevent you sleeping.

- Consider the thickness of your curtains. Have you thought about adding a thicker lining or blackout lining? If this may not be possible, for example because of the cost involved, a black plastic bag can work well as a blackout blind. It can be stapled or stuck to the curtain rail or window surround. If you use sticky Velcro, you can put this up at night and take it down during the day.

Q   **Do I try to sleep in a poor sleep environment?**

Yes   ☐   No   ☐   Sometimes   ☐

---

*It's important not to over-heat water bottles or other warming devices, and to avoid them resting directly on skin such as your feet to prevent the possibility of burns.

If you answered '*Yes*' or '*Sometimes*', these could be targets for change when you plan what you can do later.

Area 2: Altered thinking

Usually, as you try to go to sleep, your tension levels reduce, so your body and brain begin to relax and drop off to sleep. In contrast, when you're anxious, your brain becomes overly alert. You end up mulling over things again and again. This is the exact opposite of what's needed to go to sleep. Worrying thoughts are therefore both **a cause and effect** of poor sleep.

You may have anxious thoughts about life in general or specifically about not sleeping. For example:

- *Worrying about life*: You may keep mulling over things again and again, for example worrying that you may have upset someone.

- *Worrying about your sleep*: You may worry that you will not be able to sleep at all. Or that sleeplessness will reduce your ability to get through the next day. Your fears can get blown out of proportion and act to prevent you going off to sleep. Another common fear is that your brain or your body will be harmed by lack of sleep.

- Most of the time you'll find that extreme fears that you won't be able to cope at all prove untrue. It's helpful to know that not sleeping enough doesn't usually have a very big immediate effect on your brain or your body. It is possible to function well for a time with very little sleep each night. Also, when people who complain of poor sleep are asked to try to sleep in a sleep research laboratory, they may actually find they sleep more than they think. Sometimes people who are in a light level of sleep dream that they are awake. So, you may be sleeping more than you think.

Q ### Do you worry about things in general?

Yes ☐   No ☐   Sometimes ☐

Q ### Do you worry about the impact of not sleeping?

Yes ☐   No ☐   Sometimes ☐

TASK: If you answered '*Yes*' or '*Sometimes*' to either question, read the *Noticing* and *Changing unhelpful thinking* workbooks. As a first step, write down any worries about sleep on a piece of paper by your bed and mark down a day and time when you will spend time thinking through the worries in the cool light of day. Once a week review them. Remove or throw away any that did not come true. Don't focus on the worries except during the review. For specific problems, address them with the *Practical Problem solving* approach.

Area 3: Altered physical symptoms/bodily sensations

Pain, itching, breathlessness or other physical symptoms can cause sleeplessness. Tackling these physical symptoms will often help with your sleep problems.

Q ### Are physical symptoms keeping me awake?

Yes ☐   No ☐   Sometimes ☐

If you answered '*Yes*' or '*Sometimes*', please see your doctor as you may need medical treatment for your symptoms. It may be possible, for example to change the timing of water tablets (diuretics) that some people take for heart conditions. If you can take these during the day rather than just before going to sleep, it may help stop you having to get up again and again to go to the toilet. If you are being treated for fluid in your lungs, you may find that putting a raise under the two top legs of your bed raises your head and aids sleep. That can also help acid reflux, when acid tasting fluid regurgitates from your stomach and wakes you. If you notice painful acid reflux, talk to your doctor about the need for other medicines, as acid reflux can sometimes make it hard to get off, or stay asleep. If you notice symptoms of asthma gets worse while you are in bed, or you experience restless legs, or you have to get up to use the toilet more than you wish overnight, discuss these symptoms with your doctor.

Sleep apnoea is another cause of awakening from sleep and poor quality sleep. It is associated with obesity and can be caused by several factors, including obstruction to your airways as you sleep. This causes a temporary stopping of breathing and then, often, a sudden awakening. It's important that if a partner notices you seem to stop breathing for periods of time at night that this is properly evaluated medically. Speak to your doctor for their advice and assessment if you are concerned about possible sleep apnoea.

Area 4: Altered feelings/emotions

Many strong emotional feelings can be linked to sleeplessness.

Q Do you feel anxious when you try to sleep?

Yes ☐   No ☐   Sometimes ☐

If you answered '*Yes*' or '*Sometimes*', remember that anxiety is a common cause of sleeplessness. It often triggers your body's fear/fight/flight response causing adrenaline to flow. Adrenaline is a substance produced by your body that makes you feel fidgety or restless. You may notice physical symptoms such as your heartbeat and breathing getting faster, a churning feeling in your stomach or tension throughout your body. Your anxiety then acts to keep you safe and alert. This is the opposite of what you want when you're trying to fall asleep.

Q Are you feeling depressed, upset or low in mood? Or aren't you enjoying things as before?

Yes ☐   No ☐   Sometimes ☐

If you answered '*Yes*' or '*Sometimes*', remember that depression is a common cause of sleeplessness. For example when someone is feeling depressed, they may find that it takes them up to several hours to get to sleep. They may also wake up several hours earlier than normal feeling unrested or on edge. Having treatment for significant depression can often be helpful for improving your sleep.

Other emotions such as anxiety, panic, shame, guilt and anger can also cause sleeplessness.

Area 5: Altered behaviour: unhelpful behaviours

What about your sleep pattern?

If you aren't sleeping well, you can be tempted to go to bed either much earlier or much later than normal.

A regular sleep pattern can help to maintain a clear start and end to the day. Try, therefore, to get up before 9 a.m. and to sleep before about 11 p.m.

Do you have a disrupted sleep pattern (time to bed/getting up)?

Yes ☐   No ☐   Sometimes ☐

If you answered *'Yes'* or *'Sometimes'*, set yourself regular sleep times. Get up at a set time even if you have slept poorly. Try to teach your body what time to fall asleep and what time to get up. Generally, go to sleep between 11 p.m. and midnight. Try to get up at a time between 7 a.m. and 9 a.m. Adjust these times to fit your own circumstances.

NB: Try to also expose yourself to sunlight/daytime light each day by spending at least half an hour outside. This helps set your underlying sleep-wake cycle and aids sleep later in the day.

Preparing for sleep – wind-down time

The time leading up to sleep is very important. Try to build in time each evening when you relax and wind down. This might include having a bath or shower, or just spending time with a milky drink.

Physical over-activity such as exercising, eating too much, using the computer or watching TV just before going to bed can keep you awake. Sometimes people watch TV while lying in bed. This may help them wind down, but many people become more alert and so it adds to their sleep problems. Record and work out what happens for you.

Are you doing things which wake you up when you should be winding down?

Yes ☐   No ☐   Sometimes ☐

If you answered *'Yes'* or *'Sometimes'*, keep your bed as a place for sleep or for sex. Don't lie on your bed watching TV, working or worrying. This will only wake you up and prevent you sleeping.

You'll also need to decide whether listening to a radio, audiobook or music, or reading in bed helps you go to sleep. If you share a bed with someone else, discuss together how their and your night time routines affect each other's nightly wind down. Be aware that using social media or a smartphone can shine artificial light into your eyes, keeping you awake and upsetting your sleep rhythm.

Choosing not to lie in or nap

Napping during the day or sleeping in much of the morning can upset the natural sleep-wake cycle that your body needs to follow to have a good night's sleep. So, choose not to have a long nap, for example in the afternoon. And no extended lie in's each day. Once in a while is nice, for example at the weekend, but everyday naps and lies in can backfire by making you less sleepy at night.

What about caffeine?

Caffeine is a chemical found in cola drinks, coffee, tea, some hot chocolate and some herbal drinks. It causes you to be more alert. People who have lots of caffeine for several weeks can become addicted to it and notice withdrawal symptoms if they miss caffeine for a time. It also reduces your sleep quality.

Sometimes if you are really tired, consider whether you are in a pattern where you then drink more caffeine to keep alert and wake yourself up? If so, does the extra caffeine affect your sleep and worsen your tiredness?

Try not to drink more than five cups of strong coffee a day. You can switch to decaffeinated drinks or drink something else.

Q   Are you taking in too much caffeine – or drinking it too late in the day?

Yes ☐   No ☐   Sometimes ☐

If you answered *'Yes'* or *'Sometimes'*, switch slowly to decaffeinated cola, coffee or tea. Avoid drinking caffeine-containing drinks just before sleep. Some people find that a warm milky, bran-based drink can help them fall asleep.

> **KEY POINT**
>
> Caffeine stays in your body for a number of hours before it is broken down by your body or it leaves in your urine. This means that it's best to avoid drinking caffeine drinks leading up to bedtime.

What about alcohol?

Sometimes people drink alcohol to help them get to sleep. But this can actually cause problems such as unrefreshing, light sleep. Higher levels of alcohol also are known to cause anxiety, depression and sleeplessness and can worsen sleep apnoea. Drinking too much also causes people to go to the toilet more than usual at night.

Q   Am I drinking too much alcohol?

Yes ☐   No ☐   Sometimes ☐

If you answered *'Yes'* or *'Sometimes'*, plan to reduce the amount you drink before going to bed. If you drink above the healthy drink range, try to cut down in a slow step-by-step manner. Discuss how best to do this with your doctor.

Tossing, turning and clock watching

Q   Do you find yourself lying awake in bed tossing and turning, waking your partner (if you have one) up to talk (*'Are you awake?'*), or just watching the clock?

Yes ☐   No ☐   Sometimes ☐

If you answered *'Yes'* or *'Sometimes'*, then some practical changes can help such as moving the clock so you can't see it. It can still be in the room so that you can set an alarm or reach it if you have to.

How to make changes

1 **Record your sleep for a few days:**

Use your phone diary, or a paper diary such as the *Sleep diary* at the end of this workbook to identify factors that affect your sleep.

2 **Overcoming sleeplessness**

Use the checklists below to find out about things you can do to overcome your sleep problems.

Some things to do in the run-up to bed and during the day	Check here if this affects your life – even if just sometimes	Some changes you can make and resources you can use
Plan a wind-down time each evening.	☐	Choose relaxing activities, warm bran-based milky drinks may help. Consider a bath/ relaxing music.
Have a regular time to go to bed and to get up.	☐	So, you teach yourself a regular sleep-wake pattern.
Tackle the things that you know affect your sleep environment (e.g. external noise, the mattress noise).	☐	If your neighbours cause the noise, the *Practical problem solving* and *Being assertive* workbooks will help you find ways of dealing with this problem. Plan changes to your room/bed as needed.
Reduce your general life pressures.	☐	Say no – balance demands you put on yourself. Allow space and time for yourself. The *Being assertive* workbook may help you with this.
Stop, think and reflect on worrying thoughts about the past, the present and the future, and also about sleep.	☐	If worrying thoughts keep you awake, write the worries down. Decide to worry or think them through tomorrow during the day. Use the *Noticing* and *Changing unhelpful thinking* workbooks to put your thoughts into perspective the next day.
Live reasonably healthily. People who are fitter generally sleep better.	☐	It might sound strange to say this, but over-doing healthy living may become unhealthy, for example doing too much exercise. Try to live healthily but not obsessively.
Use relaxation tapes or techniques if you find them helpful.	☐	You may wish to look online for relaxing music, or try the *Tension Control* or *Slow down and Be mindfulness* resources at www.llttf.com/resources.
Drinking too much alcohol or caffeine (or smoking) just before bed.	☐	Alcohol causes sleep to be shallow and un-refreshing. It can also make you wake up more to use the toilet. Watch out for cola drinks, or too much coffee, tea or hot chocolate which can contain caffeine. Try a slow switch to decaffeinated drinks or water. Don't smoke just before bed as cigarettes and vapes cause sleeplessness too.
Doing things that stimulate you mentally or physically in the run-up to sleep (e.g. using the computer or watching an exciting film).	☐	You can, of course, do all these things, but it's advisable stop doing them at least an hour before going to bed. Avoid doing them in bed, too.

(*continued*)

Some things to do in the run-up to bed and during the day	Check here if this affects your life – even if just sometimes	Some changes you can make and resources you can use
Let problems build up so that you worry about them at night.	☐	Write down your problems to deal with at a planned time tomorrow. Many people find that their worries become a lot smaller in the light of day.
Respond in ways that end up backfiring or worsening things (e.g. napping during the day, napping beyond the time it's helpful).	☐	Try to reset your body clock by getting up at a set time each day. Try to avoid napping and go to bed at roughly the same time each day to get into a regular routine.
Don't look for answers to sleeplessness in sleeping tablets.	☐	These tablets are usually not advisable in the long-term. Speak to your doctor for their advice.

Don't expect to change everything immediately, but with practice, you can make helpful changes to your sleep pattern. If you find it hard at first, just do what you can. If you need more help, speak to your doctor.

My Review of how it goes

Afterward, even if it went well, stop and reflect on how things went. If things didn't go as you wanted, try to stop, think and reflect so you can learn from this. That way you can put what you're learning into practice so you make better and better plans going forward.

Now write down your own review:

_____

_____

_____

SUMMARY

In this workbook you have:

- Learned about sleep and sleeplessness, and the normal changes in sleeping that occur as we grow older.

- Discovered some common causes of sleep problems.

- Understood more about the pitfalls of taking sleeping tablets.

- Learned how to record your sleep pattern and identify things that can worsen your sleep.

- Discovered changes that can help you sleep better.

Before you go

What have you learned from this workbook?

_____

_____

What do you want to try next?

_____

_____

 Here are some suggested tasks to practice this approach.

Look back at the **sleep checklist of things to do and not do**. From this choose a first target to focus on. Do you want to make changes in how you prepare for sleep, what you do once you are in bed, or change things during the day?

Write down what you're going to do this week to put into practice what you have learned.

Suggested reading

Various workbooks might be helpful including _Noticing and Changing unhelpful thinking,_ and _Practical Problem solving_. Choose the workbook that you identify is most likely to help.

Worksheets to help you practice

Practice is important to help you master this approach. You can get free access to additional worksheets used in this workbook chapter and the wider book at www.llttf.com/resources

In addition, you can find a **Sleep diary** at the end of the current workbook (Figure 13.1).

Acknowledgements

The cartoon illustrations were produced by Keith Chan, kchan75@hotmail.com. Thank you to Mrs Theresa Kelly and Mrs Sue Wood at Five Areas Ltd for their helpful advice and comments on earlier drafts of this book. Also, to those practitioners and Peer mentors at North West Senior and Disability Services in Oregon, USA who inputted into the initial modifications of these resources to suit an older adult readership.

The term Five Areas® is a registered trademark of Five Areas Resources Ltd. Although we hope you find this book helpful, it's not intended to be a direct substitute for consultative advice with a healthcare professional, nor do we give any assurance about its effectiveness in a particular case. Accordingly, neither we nor the author shall be held liable for any loss or damages arising from its use.

My Sleep Diary

Time when you are in bed and trying to sleep	Record when you are/were asleep with a 'X'	When in bed, record any thoughts/images that go through your mind and keep you awake (for example worries, fears about sleeping or the impact of not sleeping).
8.00 p.m.– 9.59 p.m.		
10.00 p.m. – 11.59 p.m.		
12.00 a.m. – 1.59 a.m.		
2.00 a.m. – 3.59 a.m.		
4.00 a.m. – 5.59 a.m.		
6.00 a.m. – 7.59 a.m.		
8.00 a.m. – 9.59 a.m.		
10.00 a.m. – 11.59 a.m.		
12.00 p.m. – 1.59 p.m.		
2.00 p.m. – 3.59 p.m.		
4.00 p.m. – 5.59 p.m.		
6:00 p.m. – 7:59 p.m.		

Record any activities you do that relate to sleep

Before bed: alcohol, caffeine, smoking, exercise, daytime napping, computer games, watching scary films, sleeping in, etc.

In bed: reading, audiobooks, social media, sex, listening to the radio, noises like snoring or conversations with a partner, tossing/turning, getting up and going downstairs, etc.

Figure 13.1 My Sleep Diary

Overcoming Depression and Low Mood in Older Adults

A Five Areas® CBT Approach

Harmful drinking and you

Dr Chris Williams

DOI: 10.4324/9781003347637-19

Do you ever notice this?

My daughter wants me to just stop drinking

I'm starting to need a drink each day

What's wrong with a drink at night?

It makes me feel relaxed

I just can't sleep

I'm older and have no reason not to drink

I feel I'm living a lie

People like me when I'm drinking

I've no confidence if I don't have a drink

I'm in control of it – I don't have a problem

I feel completely trapped

Is this you?

If so, … this workbook is for you.

In this workbook you will learn:

- Some useful facts about harmful drinking.

- How alcohol can unhelpfully affect you and your family.

- What effects drink is having on you.

- Some things you can do to bring about change if you have a problem.

Introduction

In England, around 1.5-2 million people have alcohol dependence. If you are abusing and dependent on alcohol you have a serious problem that usually needs medical help.

A far higher number – around 11 million people drink at a level that causes them harm (https://www.gov.uk/government/publications/health-matters-harmful-drinking-and-alcohol-dependence/health-matters-harmful-drinking-and-alcohol-dependence).

Alcohol is widely used socially – for fun, relaxation and enjoyment. But it can cause major problems, especially if you drink regularly and over a prolonged time. As you get older, your body and brain may not be able to tolerate and process alcohol in the same way as they did when younger. This can lead to greater risks of harm than before.

This workbook is especially focused on people who are drinking at a potentially harmful level.

Using alcohol

Alcohol is widely used – and is often seen as part of a good night out with friends. It may often become part of your evening or weekend routine – to wind down, relax or even get to sleep.

Surveys show that **many people have drinking problems**. These often start when people use alcohol to help them get through the day or week.

Have you been drinking to:

- Fit in with the crowd?

- Block out uncomfortable feelings or physical symptoms?

- Relax?

- Cheer yourself up?

- Get off to sleep?

If you regularly drink more than the recommended alcohol levels for weeks or months it can affect your mood, body and relationships. It can also worsen depression and anxiety.

Many doctors recommend that the highest levels of alcohol for adults to drink in one week should be:

- 14 units for women.

- 14 units for men.

A unit of alcohol is around the amount of alcohol that the average adult can process and remove from their body in an hour.

The amounts are less (and sometimes much less) for much younger people and older adults depending on their age and weight. Likewise, if you have a smaller build, or are older, poorly, or on medication, the amount you can drink before your intake becomes harmful will vary.

What is a unit of alcohol?

1 unit = half a pint of lower strength lager/beer, or 1 small glass of wine (125 ml glass of 13% ABV), or one shot of spirits (e.g. 25 ml of 40% ABV vodka, whisky or gin).

A standard glass of wine (175 ml glass) is typically 2.3 units or 3.3 units for a large glass of wine (250 ml).

These values vary because stronger beers or wines contain far more than one unit of alcohol.

(https://www.gov.uk/government/publications/health-matters-harmful-drinking-and-alcohol-dependence/health-matters-harmful-drinking-and-alcohol-dependence).

The recommended maximum level of drink of 14 units a week look like:

6 medium glasses of wine

6 pints of ordinary strength beer/lager/cider.

Or 14 single measures of spirit.

To find out more, visit www.alcoholchange.org.uk, or visit your GP.

KEY POINT

Always look at the back of the bottle, where you'll find how much alcohol there is in standard-size glasses for that particular drink.

In many ways, the key is whether you are experiencing *harmful drinking*. If you are, no matter how many units you drink a week, it's important to cut back.

One challenge with drinking is it's easy to overlook or play down what you drink. The only way to be sure is to keep a diary and record what you drink over a week.

TASK: A good first step is to record how much you drink. Remember that most people tend to think they have a lot less than they really have.

Recording your drinking

The best way of finding out how much you drink or use in a week is to keep a **diary**.

How much alcohol did you drink?

In the last day:

* What drink?   ___

* How much?   ___

* How many times?   ___

In the last week?

* What drink?   ___

* How much?   ___

* How many times?   ___

* How many units is that per week?   ___

* How much are you spending a week on drinks?   ___

Try to **record each and every time** you drink alcohol. Use the *Drink diary* (Figure 14.1) to help you do this. At the end of the week, add up the amount and cost of what you have spent and drunk.

A further copy of the drink diary is available at the end of this workbook (Figure 14.2).

How alcohol affects you

When you drink a large amount of alcohol – or regularly drink at lower levels – you can be harmed. Some of these harmful effects are described below.

Thinking/psychological harm

A **Problems caused by the people and events around us**.

People often drink or use drugs to improve how they feel. But actually, too much alcohol can cause anxiety and depressed mood, and prevent depression from getting better.

Drinking can also:

* Increase worry and panic attacks.

* Lead to confusion or violence.

* Damage your concentration and memory so that you find it hard to learn and remember new information.

* Impact your ability to fall asleep and to have a refreshing night's sleep.

* Cause you to become fearful, increasingly suspicious and mistrustful of others.

* Lead to addiction with craving if you drink at a higher level for long enough.

Day and date	Morning	Afternoon	Evening	Total units and cost
Monday				Total units/amount per day= Cost/day =
Tuesday				Total units/amount per day= Cost/day =
Wednesday				Total units/amount per day= Cost/day =
Thursday				Total units/amount per day= Cost/day =
Friday				Total units/amount per day= Cost/day =
Saturday				Total units/amount per day= Cost/day =
Sunday				Total units/amount per day= Cost/day =
Weekly total				

Figure 14.1 Drink Diary of what you drink

Drinking can also make you feel irritable. Your personality can change, but often in such a subtle way that you don't realise at first that you're changing as a result of a habit. You may become withdrawn and stop taking interest in other people or the things around you. You could even become suspicious of everything around you.

People can occasionally develop severe psychiatric (mental health) disorders that can become long term such as having hallucinations (seeing or hearing things that other people do not hear or see) or delusions (beliefs that don't reflect reality). Alcohol can also cause or worsen dementia (alcoholic dementia).

Q Do you have any of the mental health symptoms described above? (Note: You may need to ask people around you.)

Yes ☐   No ☐   Sometimes ☐

Physical changes

- The most common symptom of drinking too much is having a hangover. You may feel sick with headaches and feel dehydrated.

- If you drink a lot of alcohol, you can become physically as well as psychologically dependent on them.

- If someone drinks at a high level for some time and then suddenly stops taking them, there is a high risk of **withdrawal symptoms**. This is a serious medical condition. Symptoms of withdrawal may include sweating, feeling sick, confused, agitated and experiencing hallucinations. The person can go into a coma, have seizures or wet themselves.

- Alcohol causes damage to different parts of your body. For example, it can cause stomach ulcers (damage to the lining of your stomach) and damage your liver. It can also damage your brain leading to epileptic seizures or cause alcoholic dementia. Other important body organs such as the pancreas can also be damaged; causing pain. Alcohol can also increase the risk of cancer.

Q Do you have any of the physical symptoms described above?

Yes ☐   No ☐   Sometimes ☐

Social changes

- When regular high levels of drinking takes hold, it can have a powerful impact on how you live your life. You may find you start to forget your values and ideals of how you want to live, and the drinking can become the most important thing in your life. Other important people and commitments get pushed out as a result.

- You may have problems at home such as **arguments** with family and friends.

- You may get into **debt**.

- You may struggle to keep up at work (if you still work) – or at home. You may ignore or neglect people you care about such as your partner, children, grandchildren, friends or pets.

- **Accidents and violence** are also common social consequences of alcohol and drug dependency.

Q **Do you have any of the social changes described above?**

Yes ☐   No ☐   Sometimes ☐

Based on your answers to all the questions above:

Q **Overall, do you think that you're experiencing a drinking problem?**

Yes ☐   No ☐   Sometimes ☐

If you have answered "*Yes*" or "*Sometimes*" to this question, then this is an alert that you need to make some changes.

KEY POINT

Drinking in ways that can harm you or others is likely to cause you increasing problems in each of the areas described above. *You need to tackle your problem now.* Don't be tempted to downplay or ignore things and believe it isn't a problem. *Ignoring things is often part of the problem.*

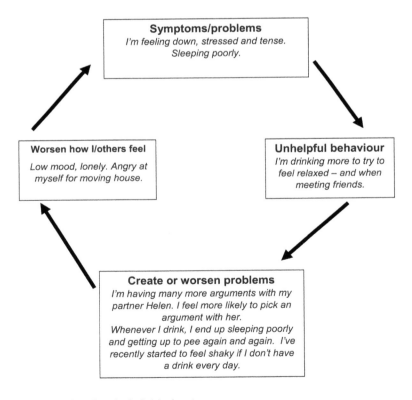

Figure 14.2 Paul's vicious cycle of unhelpful behaviour

In the short term:

- *Physically*: Paul is noticing he feels *shaky* if he doesn't have a drink every day.

- *Psychologically*: He thinks drink makes him more relaxed and helps him sleep at night. But then he wakes up and has to go to the toilet. So, he *feels too tired to get up in the morning* and *sleeps in* to catch up on sleep. This impacts his sleeping pattern. He also feels more depressed in the morning when he's been drinking the night before.

- *Socially*: *Paul's partner, Helen, is worried about him.* They keep *having arguments* about this. Paul knows it's damaging their relationship.

 KEY POINT

Both *helpful* and *unhelpful* behaviours can make us feel better in the short term. But in the longer term, our unhelpful behaviours such as harmful drinking backfires. It impacts on how we or others feel. It becomes part of our problem.

The good news is that if this applies to you, you can make changes.

What about you?

How does your drinking affect you and the people around you in the short term and longer term?

Short term

Physically?

_____

_____

Psychologically?

_____

_____

Socially (on you and others - for example, your family, children or friends)?

_____

_____

Longer term (look back over the past six to 12 months)

i **Physically?**

_____

_____

ii **Psychologically?**

_____

_____

iii **Socially (on you and others)?**

_____

_____

If after reading this workbook you have discovered that your drinking is causing harm to you or others, then **you need to tackle it**.

If you're drinking at a far higher level

If you stop drinking too quickly, you may notice symptoms of withdrawal. This is probably the reason why so many people don't manage to tackle this problem. But it's possible to make changes – and it's even more important to do so if you're drinking a lot.

To successfully change your drinking, you need to cut down the amount you're taking in a slow **step-by-step manner**. You may find the *Unhelpful things you do* workbook can be helpful for some ideas of how to plan this. But if you're drinking alcohol at higher levels, it's best to make these changes together with some closer help and advice from your GP, therapist, or your local drug or alcohol support services.

Before you start, discuss your goals and how to achieve this with your doctor.

How to plan changes

Try to reduce your overall intake of alcohol each week:

- Do this slowly in steady steps over several weeks.

- Make some slow, steady reductions in the number of units you drink. Slow down your drinking. Switch to soft or virgin drinks every other drink.

- In the short term it may help you if you limit the times you go out to drink or how much alcohol you buy in at home.

- If possible, at a minimum, plan to eventually have at least **two days** each week without any drink to allow your body to recover.

1 **My Plan:**

Think about your plans over the next few weeks and months.

Q What are you going to aim for first?

_____

_____

_____

Q Do you need to break this target down into smaller steps?

_____

_____

_____

If so, write your revised target here:

_____

2 **What am I going to do?**

_____

3 **When am I going to do it?**

_____

4 **IS MY PLANNED TASK:**

_____

Q Useful for understanding or changing how I am?

Yes ☐   No ☐

Q Clear and specific, so that I will know when I have done it?

Yes ☐   No ☐

Q Realistic, practical and achievable?

Yes ☐   No ☐

Q What problems or difficulties could arise – and how could I overcome these?

_____

_____

Now, carry out your plan

Try to do your plan anyway. Good luck!

My Review of how it went

Afterward, even if it went well, stop and reflect on how things went. If things didn't go as you wanted, try to stop, think and reflect so you can learn from this. That way you can put what you're learning into practice so you make better and better plans going forward.

- What went well?

- What didn't go so well?

- How can you take what you've learned so you make better and better plans going forward?

Now write down your own review:

_____

_____

By building one small change upon another, you can slowly cut down your drinking both outside and inside your home.

SUMMARY

In this workbook you have learned:

- Some useful facts about harmful drinking.

- How alcohol can unhelpfully affect you and your family.

- What effects drink is having on you.

- Some things you can do to bring about change if you have a problem.

Before you go

What have you learned from this workbook?

_____

_____

What do you want to try *next*?

_____

_____

_____

(**try it out!**)

You are likely to make the most progress if you can act on what you have learned in the workbook. It may be tempting to put it off. It may be really hard to change because of the grip that drinking has on you. That's when you need extra help. Ask your doctor about local supports such as *Alcoholics Anonymous* and local *Drug and Alcohol services*.

Worksheets to help you practice

Practice is important to help you master this approach. A further copy of a Drink diary follows at the end of the workbook (Figure 14.2). You can get free access to additional worksheets used in this workbook chapter and wider book at www.llttf.com/resources

Acknowledgements

The cartoon illustrations were produced by Keith Chan, kchan75@hotmail.com. Thank you to Mrs Theresa Kelly and Mrs Sue Wood at Five Areas Ltd for their helpful advice and comments on earlier drafts of this book. Also, to those practitioners and Peer mentors at North West Senior and Disability Services in Oregon, USA who inputted into the initial modifications of these resources to suit an older adult readership.

Day and date	Morning	Afternoon	Evening	Total units and cost
Monday				Total units/amount per day= Cost/day =
Tuesday				Total units/amount per day= Cost/day =
Wednesday				Total units/amount per day= Cost/day =
Thursday				Total units/amount per day= Cost/day =
Friday				Total units/amount per day= Cost/day =
Saturday				Total units/amount per day= Cost/day =
Sunday				Total units/amount per day= Cost/day =
Weekly total				

Drink Diary of what you drink

Overcoming Depression and Low Mood in Older Adults

A Five Areas® CBT approach

Understanding and using antidepressant medication

Dr Chris Williams

DOI: 10.4324/9781003347637-20

Do you ever notice this?

Is this you?

If so, … this workbook is for you.

In this workbook you will:

- Find out about how antidepressants are used to treat a medical diagnosis of clinical depression and some other disorders.

- Get the answers to some common questions about antidepressants.

- Get some useful hints and tips to get the best out of medication if your doctor has prescribed this.

- Learn how to think through the advantages and disadvantages of taking medication, if this is being recommended to you as an appropriate treatment.

How do medicines fit in with your treatment?

Antidepressant medication can be helpful as part of a **package of care**. National Treatment Guidelines often recommend that people with depression should be offered treatments such as psychological or 'talking' treatments as well as approaches such as medication. They can both be equal parts of a package of care.

Your doctor can tell you more about the different types of antidepressants available.

KEY POINT

If you've already been prescribed an antidepressant, you should continue to take them as originally planned, and all your treatment decisions should be made with your doctor.

When are antidepressant medicines helpful?

Antidepressants are at their most helpful if you experience moderate or severe symptoms of depression. This is sometimes called **clinical depression** – a situation where symptoms are having a major effect on your life.

Symptoms of clinical depression often include:

- Feeling low or noticing you no longer enjoy things most of the time for at least two weeks.

- Several physical changes of depression (e.g. low energy, reduced concentration, changes in your sleep pattern or appetite).

- Feeling agitated, suspicious or panicky.

- Sometimes noticing suicidal ideas, where you can't see a future.

Some other times when antidepressants may be used

Besides clinical depression, antidepressants are also sometimes used to treat other mental and physical health problems. For example:

- Anxiety and tension.

- Panic attacks.

- Physical symptoms such as chronic fatigue (feeling tired all the time), fibromyalgia (pain in your muscles and joints) and general body aches.

- Obsessive-compulsive disorder (OCD) and social phobia.

KEY POINT

If antidepressants are recommended, ask your doctor the reason why you may be prescribed an antidepressant, and how long you might need to take them.

Your attitude towards medication

If tablets of any type are recommended by your doctor, your beliefs and attitudes towards taking them can affect whether you choose to take the tablets or not. We can all have different attitudes towards medication. Consider your own attitudes towards taking antidepressant medication.

I think I should get better on my own without taking pills

KEY POINT

Remember, our body, thoughts and feelings are all part of us – they are not in separate boxes. If you break your leg, you are unlikely to say *'I want to get better by myself without medical treatment'*. So why do this if you're experiencing depression? If your doctor recommends that you take antidepressants, discuss why they are suggesting this. You should jointly make the decision about whether it's the right thing for you at the moment.

Taking antidepressant medication can be one of the several ways of helping yourself to get better. They can helpfully change some of the physical symptoms that accompany clinical depression and can improve how you feel, improve your confidence in how you relate to others and help you start to become more active. However, taking pills doesn't replace the need for you to work at changing other things in your life such as tackling relationship problems or other practical problems such as debt.

My family and friends are unhappy I'm taking antidepressants

Sometimes people can have strong views about antidepressant medications. As in the example above about the broken leg, the helpful advice they could offer is that if your doctor suggests a treatment that is seen as good medical practice, you would be best advised to try it if you are struggling. Treatment won't always mean taking pills, although medication can often be an important part of your overall treatment package. If friends or family continue to be unhappy, perhaps you could ask them to come with you to discuss their concerns with your own doctor.

Frequently asked questions

 ## Why do doctors use antidepressant medication for treating depression?

Remember in the Five Areas® Model: in *low mood and depression,* there are links between the changes in your thinking, feelings, behaviour and your body. Because of the links among each of the areas, the **physical treatment** offered by medication can lead to improvements in the other areas too.

 ## How well do antidepressants work?

About half to two-thirds of people who have severe or moderate depression find that taking antidepressants helps lift their symptoms.

 ## How long do they take to work?

Don't expect immediate results. Antidepressant medicines can take up to two to four weeks or more to begin to work. And it may take longer for their maximum benefit to show.

Therefore, it's very important that you take the pills regularly and for long enough, even if to begin with they seem like they aren't working. Sometimes, doctors advise a low dose to start with. This can be slowly increased over several weeks/months if needed.

 KEY POINT

You shouldn't give up on your antidepressant medicine if you don't notice changes.

 ## Do antidepressant medications always work in the end?

Like most medicines, not everyone can tolerate antidepressant tablets or wants to take them. Even when taken at the recommended dose for long enough, not everyone notices the benefits of these tablets. Doctors have recommended next steps to take if improvement does not come. Typically, this can include increasing the dose of medication, switching to another type of antidepressant, taking additional tablets alongside the antidepressant, or adding additional treatments. This might include seeing a specialist psychiatrist or having an additional therapy such as cognitive behavioural therapy (CBT) alongside the prescribed medication. Talk to your doctor so you understand the options available to you.

 ## Do antidepressants have side effects?

All medications have side effects. That is true of commonly taken medications such as aspirin and paracetamol as well as antidepressants. The important question is whether the side effects of having untreated depression are worse. Often, a pragmatic approach would be to test out the advantages or disadvantages of taking tablets in your own experience.

Many side effects improve within a few days of starting the pills as your body gets used to them. Your doctor should have gone through the possible side effects with you when you started treatment. But you can always ask again if you are unsure. You should also read the patient information leaflet that comes with every prescription.

Q ### Can I drive or use machinery if I take pills?

Many antidepressant medications affect your ability to drive and operate machinery. They can often also increase the effects of alcohol. Read the patient information leaflet that you would have received with your prescription to see if this applies to you. Or, ask your doctor if you have any doubts.

Q ### Are antidepressants addictive?

Antidepressants are **not** addictive in the same way that some other drugs are such as benzodiazepines, but stopping them all at once may still cause you to notice unpleasant symptoms.

Because of this, when you are ready to stop taking the pills, your doctor may suggest you taper down the dose over several weeks or months. Again, the best thing is to discuss these issues with your prescribing doctor.

Practical problems you may have while taking medication

Remembering to take your pills

It can be hard to remember to take any medication on a regular basis. It's even harder when depression worsens your concentration.

You may find it helpful to:

- Organise your tablets. Many are held in bubble packs that state the day or time of day to take the medication.

- Get into a routine. Take the medication at a set time each day.

- Many pharmacies sell plastic pillboxes (sometimes called dosette boxes) that have compartments for each day and part of the day into which you can place the correct dose of pills. That way you will know when you have taken them.

- Place the medicines somewhere you will see them when you need to take them, for example by your toothbrush. Use coloured pieces of paper to remind you if you don't want other people to read your notes.

- Set an alarm on your watch, an alarm clock or the alarm function on a phone or personal assistant device to remind you to take pills at a set time.

- Ask other people to remind you/phone you if you find that you struggle to remember otherwise.

- **Please note**: Medications can be dangerous if taken in overdose or by mistake.

Keep them safely away from children.

I sometimes take a higher dose than is prescribed

It may be tempting to take extra pills at times of higher distress to cope even when your doctor hasn't prescribed the medicine with this in mind. The danger is that taking higher doses may cause nasty side effects and potentially be dangerous. There can also be unexpected problems and interactions with other medications you take.

KEY POINT

Taking more medicine than your doctor has told you to take can backfire and worsen how you feel. This is because taking medicines at higher than recommended doses may cause you to have unpleasant side effects. It may be dangerous and also it wrongly teaches you that you're only managing to cope because of using the extra medication. You then come to believe that you can't live life without the medicine.

Stopping antidepressants

Sometimes people can be tempted to stop taking medication without telling their doctor. You may be afraid you are letting them down or that you will be 'told off' if you do. But it's actually better to discuss any worries you have openly with them. It's often important when stopping antidepressants to do this gradually by agreeing to a timetable with your doctor. This reduces the chances of noticing discontinuation symptoms as a result of stopping the medication in one go.

KEY POINT

Stopping an antidepressant too early is one of the causes of worsening depression. Many doctors advise their patients to continue to take the antidepressant medication for at least six months after feeling better to prevent slipping back into depression.

Putting things into practice

If you want to find out more about the use of antidepressant medications, please discuss this with your doctor. They will be able to suggest other sources of information about the treatments that are available.

SUMMARY

In this workbook you have learned:

- How antidepressants are used to treat a medical diagnosis of clinical depression and some other disorders.

- The answers to some common questions about antidepressants.

- Some useful hints and tips to get the best out of medication if your doctor has prescribed this.

- The advantages and disadvantages of taking medication, if this is being recommended to you as an appropriate treatment.

Before you go

What have you learned from this workbook?

_____

_____

What do you want to try next?

_____

_____

 Here are some suggested tasks to practice this approach.

Think about what the main issues are for you concerning antidepressant medication. You might need more information, want to discuss starting, changing or stopping medication or perhaps consider how to better manage side effects.

Worksheets to help you practice

Practice is important to help you master this approach. You can get free access to additional worksheets used in the wider book at www.llttf.com/resources

Acknowledgements

The cartoon illustrations were produced by Keith Chan, kchan75@hotmail.com. Thank you to Mrs Theresa Kelly and Mrs Sue Wood at Five Areas Ltd for their helpful advice and comments on earlier drafts of this book. Also, to those practitioners and Peer mentors at North West Senior and Disability Services in Oregon, USA who inputted into the initial modifications of these resources to suit an older adult readership.

The term Five Areas® is a registered trademark of Five Areas Resources Ltd. Although we hope you find this book helpful, it's not intended to be a direct substitute for consultative advice with a healthcare professional, nor do we give any assurance about its effectiveness in a particular case. Accordingly, neither we nor the author shall be held liable for any loss or damages arising from its use

PART 6

Planning for the future

Overcoming Depression and Low Mood in Older Adults

A Five Areas® CBT Approach

Planning for the future

Dr Chris Williams

DOI: 10.4324/9781003347637-22

Do you ever notice this?

Is this you?

If so, … this workbook is for you.

Introduction

This workbook is designed to be read as you come to the end of working on improving how you feel.

In this workbook you will:

- Look back at what you have learned while working on getting better.

- Summarise key lessons you have learned.

- Make a clear plan to stay well.

- Set up some review days so you can check your own progress.

- Work out 'danger signs' that will alert you that things may be slipping back. Then plan what to do if that happens.

The journey of recovery

It can sometimes be helpful to think of yourself as being on a **journey through life**. At times that journey seems happy, relaxed and fun. At other times it seems harder. Maybe at times, we feel lonely or it's a struggle. We slip up, or struggle at times of illness or low energy. This whole wider course contains workbook resources that teach various helpful life skills that can make a difference. Hopefully over recent weeks and months, as you have worked and applied what you've read, you have noticed some benefits in how you feel.

In the following sections, there are some questions to help you identify **what has helped you**.

My journey

Q What is different now from before?

_____

_____

Q What gains have you made?

_____

_____

How have things changed/improved in each of the Five Areas®?

Area 1: Situations, relationships and practical problems

Q How have things changed/improved in the situations and practical problems you face?

_____

_____

Q What practical resources have you discovered in yourself and in the support from others around you? (For example how to build close relationships?)

_____

_____

Area 2: Altered thinking

Q How have things changed/improved in your thinking?

_____

_____

Areas 3 and 4: Altered feelings/physical symptoms and sensations

Q How have things changed/improved in your feelings and the physical symptoms you used to have? (For example you may still have the same worries and fears but not be troubled by them as often.)

_____

_____

Area 5: Altered behaviour or activity levels

Q How have things changed/improved in your behaviour and activity levels? What can you do now and what can't you still do? If there are activities you can't do because of age or illness, have you managed to plan elements of some of them into your life – whether it is competition, exercise, socialising or more?

Have you overcome any areas of avoidance?

Or have you built up activities that you enjoy, becoming aware of your achievements, or connecting more with people you like?

Do you now respond to things in more helpful or unhelpful ways? Are you more likely to make choices that reflect the person you want to be?

_____

_____

Working out what's made the difference

Q What have you done to make these changes happen?

_____

_____

Q What new skills have you gained that you can use to help you continue to improve?

_____

_____

What practical steps can you take to continue making changes?

Some things you could choose to do

> **EXAMPLE: ANNE'S MENTAL FITNESS PLAN**
>
> - _'When I begin to feel low and stressed, I need to do something about it before it worsens'._
>
> - _'Don't withdraw from others when I feel down – they can really help me feel better'._
>
> - _'When I feel overwhelmed by problems – just tackle them one at a time'._

Checklist: some possible helpful responses to maintain improvement

Some things that can help:	Check here if you have discovered this helpful – and want to keep doing this activity
Tackle things early if you feel worse. Build on your strengths/resources.	☐
Stop, think and reflect on unhelpful thoughts. Don't let extreme and unhelpful thinking take over.	☐
Keep doing things that improve how you feel emotionally and physically (i.e. those activities that you value and give a sense of pleasure, achievement and closeness/connection to other people).	☐

(continued)

Some things that can help:	Check here if you have discovered this helpful – and want to keep doing this activity
Keep physically active, getting up regularly when you have sat for 30–60 minutes. Walking briskly so you get slightly short of breath. Taking the stairs when you can. Doing some strength exercises during each week. Seek advice from your doctor or physiotherapist as to what levels of exercise are appropriate for you.	☐
Face up to your fears – don't let avoidance take over.	☐
Live reasonably healthily – being active, eating, sleeping – but not obsessively so.	☐
Say 'No' – balance demands you put on yourself. Allow space and time for you. Be assertive.	☐
Use relaxation or meditation tapes or techniques if you find them helpful. You can download these from www.llttf.com/resources	☐
If you are prescribed an anti-depressant medication, take it regularly and as prescribed. Discuss any changes you want to make with your own doctor.	☐

Some responses that can be less helpful:	Check here if this is something you have discovered makes you feel worse emotionally or physically
Letting problems build up and not dealing with them.	☐
Letting unhelpful thinking spiral out of control.	☐
Avoiding things or putting things off. Remember the less you do, the worse you feel.	☐
Acting in ways that backfire/worsen things (e.g. taking on too much or setting yourself up to fail).	☐
Drinking too much or blocking how you feel using street drugs. Misusing medication – for example taking extra doses that aren't prescribed.	☐

Q   What else have I learned about getting and staying better?

_____

_____

Staying well: Watching out for the problem times

One important thing is to watch out for problem times that suggest you are struggling. If you do this, you can plan in advance what you're going to do if you start to feel worse for whatever reason.

This could happen when you experience:

- Personal loss: When you feel let down, rejected or abandoned by someone, for example lose a friendship or experience a bereavement.

- Setbacks or challenges: For example illness or loss of independence. Changes of many types such as retirement, a house move or children or others moving away, can affect how we feel.

- Stress: When you think things are beginning to get out of control. For example it's common for people who have been in the hospital for some time to find it stressful when they first return home. Or if costs increase, and our pension or income doesn't keep pace.

KEY POINT

The key is not to think that you need to avoid these problem times. Instead, the challenge is to find ways of responding that will help you either sort out a practical problem or feel more resilient and able to cope.

Q **In which situations are you most likely to have setbacks?**

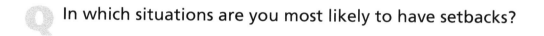

_____

_____

Q **What can you do differently if you encounter these situations?**

_____

_____

EXAMPLE: **Anne identifies her early warning signs**

   i. Situations, relationships and practical problems:

   - Feeling overwhelmed by problems and not acting to overcome them.

  ii. Altered thinking:

   - Becoming very negative and predicting that things will go badly (*negative predictions*); having a very negative view of myself (*bias against yourself*); overlooking good things that happen (*negative mental filter*); worrying too much about things that might go wrong (*catastrophising*).

 iii. Altered feelings:

   - Feeling low and weepy, and also feeling very little at all as though my feelings are becoming numb.

 iv. Altered physical feelings/symptoms:

   - Feeling very low in energy and finding it hard to get up in the morning. Noticing my sleep patterns worsening.

v. Altered behaviour/activity levels:

- A tendency to want to avoid and withdraw and ask my sister not to visit. Stopping doing things I normally enjoy such as reading and sitting on the bench in the park. Starting to snack more when I feel stressed.

What about you? Your own early warning signs

Now make your list of early warning signs:

Area 1: Situations, relationships and practical problems

_____

_____

Area 2: Altered thinking

_____

_____

Area 3: Altered feelings/emotions

_____

_____

Area 4: Altered physical symptoms/sensations

_____

_____

Area 5: Altered behaviour/activity levels

_____

_____

EXAMPLE: Anne identifies one key early warning sign:

I am going to watch out for times when I start to avoid people by staying in and not answering the phone.

This key early warning sign means: Do something now to tackle how I feel.

Write in Your own key early warning sign(s):

_____

_____

Making an emergency plan

An emergency plan refers to a plan you can put into action if you notice you are feeling worse.

Imagine one day you hear a smoke alarm beeping while you're in bed. What do you do? **Do you ignore it** and lie there as if there was no problem? Or do you get up to try to deal with it?

 KEY POINT

You need to have planned what you do in response to your key early warning signs.

This could include doing the activities you already summarised in the *Some possible helpful responses to maintain improvement checklist* earlier in this workbook on pages 217–8.

For example you could:

- **Respond helpfully**. Keep doing things that you value and see as important. Things that give you a sense of pleasure, achievement or closeness to others. Maintain your healthy, helpful habits. Do what has helped you before. Try to make choices that allow you to live your life as you want to.

- **Choose to stay in contact with people who support you**. Don't isolate yourself – tell others you trust if you are experiencing problems.

- If you are struggling, talk to a healthcare practitioner and discuss whether you need more help.

- Create an **emergency plan** to help you to tackle any early warning signs you notice. The following example shows how Anne decides to react to her early warning signs.

 EXAMPLE: Anne's emergency plan

Altered thinking: With unhelpful thinking and mind-reading.	I need to identify and challenge unhelpful thinking.
Altered feelings: Feeling low and weepy.	Do the things in the table, – and also go to see my doctor to talk about whether other help may be useful.
Altered physical symptoms/bodily sensations: Feeling low in energy and worse in the morning.	Plan to do more difficult tasks later on in the day when I feel better. Do things at a level I can cope with.
Altered behaviour: Withdrawing from doing things I like.	Create an action plan to do things that give me a sense of pleasure, closeness/connection to people I like and recognise my achievements. Remember to make choices that reflect my values/things I see as important.
Altered behaviour: Asking my sister not to visit.	Choose to ask my sister to come over each week for a visit. If it seems hard explain why I need to keep the visits short.

Now, create your own emergency response plan.

Q **What is your emergency plan in case you have a setback?**

Try to be very clear about **what** you will do and **when** you will do it. Include responses you will do, as well as any people you could contact to ask for help. Going back to the example of the smoke alarm used earlier – if a fire was beginning to worsen at home in spite of your attempts to tackle it, you would call for professional help. Similarly, if you feel worse in spite of your emergency plan, you should get in touch with someone who can help like a health professional. They can advise you whether other approaches may be helpful.

_____

_____

To help you detect set backs, and keep responding so you stay well, you can plan a **Review day.**

Plan a regular review day

Every week, why not choose a day in your calendar as a '_Review Day_'? If this feels too often, try to do this at least once a month – perhaps on the last day of the month so you can look at and review your progress. During this Review time, try to spend 30 minutes or so thinking back over things since your last review.

Here are some ideas about how to go about your review.

- Complete a blank _Five Areas® Assessment_ (you can get more at www.llttf.com/resources). Check how you are doing in each area. Any progress? Any set-backs? Do you need to re-read or work on any new areas? Do you need extra advice/help?

_____

_____

- What's gone well – and less well?

_____

_____

- Are you struggling or slipping back (review your warning signs list or emergency plan if needed)?

_____

_____

- What can you learn from what has happened?

_____

_____

_____

- How can you put what has been learned into practice?

_____

_____

_____

1 **My Plan:**

Now, based on this review, think about your plans over the next few weeks and months.

Q What are you going to do next?

_____

_____

Q Do you need to break those targets down into smaller steps?

Once you have a clear first target, write your own plan here:

2 **What am I going to do?**

_____

3 **When am I going to do it?**

_____

4 **IS MY PLANNED TASK:**

Q Useful for understanding or changing how I am?

Yes ☐   No ☐

Q Clear and specific, so that I will know when I have done it?

Yes ☐   No ☐

Q Realistic, practical and achievable?

Yes ☐   No ☐

Q What problems or difficulties could arise – and how could I overcome these?

_____

_____

Now, carry out your plan

Try to do your plan anyway. Good luck!

My Review of how it went

Afterward, even if it went well, stop and reflect on how things went. If things didn't go as you wanted, try to stop, think and reflect so you can learn from this. That way you can put what you're learning into practice so you make better and better plans going forward.

Now write down your own review:

_____

_____

Sources of extra help

- **Your family doctor.** Your doctor can offer medical advice and (if they feel it is necessary) refer you to a mental health specialist for a detailed assessment.

- **Social services.** Social services can be a great source of support for families. You can find your local social services office hours' phone number and a 24-hour emergency phone number in local directories or online.

SUMMARY

In this workbook you have:

- Looked back at what you have learned while working on getting better.

- Summarised key lessons you have learned.

- Made a clear plan to stay well.

- Set up some Review days so you can check your own progress.

- Worked out 'danger signs' that will alert you that things may be slipping back. Then planned what to do if that happens.

Before you go

What have you learned from this workbook?

_____

_____

What do you want to try next?

_____

_____

You are likely to make the most progress and build on the progress you have made if you keep putting into practice what you have learned about improving how you feel. This workbook contains various suggestions – a plan to cope, watching for signs you are slipping back, and creating an emergency plan.

Suggested task

Whatever you choose to do, try to maintain the underlying pattern of *Plan, Do and Review* throughout the week and month. Keep reflecting on how things are going, giving yourself a pat on the back when things go well, and being gentle on yourself if you have a set-back. Remember you're not on your own, many millions of people experience low mood at some time in life, and through workbooks like these, through families and friends as well as through health care professionals, help is at hand.

Worksheets to help you practice

Practice is important to help you master this approach. You can get free access to additional worksheets used in this workbook chapter and wider book at www.llttf.com/resources

A request for feedback

Finally, you've now finished the workbooks. Well done! I hope it's been helpful. The contents of the Five Areas® workbooks are updated and improved on a regular basis. If there are areas in the workbooks that you found hard to understand or that seemed unclear or confusing, please let us know via the Contact Us form at www.llttf.com/contact.

Acknowledgements

The cartoon illustrations were produced by Keith Chan, kchan75@hotmail.com. Thank you to Mrs Theresa Kelly and Mrs Sue Wood at Five Areas Ltd for their helpful advice and comments on earlier drafts of this book. Also, to those practitioners and Peer mentors at North West Senior and Disability Services in Oregon, USA who inputted into the initial modifications of these resources to suit an older adult readership.

The term Five Areas® is a registered trademark of Five Areas Resources Ltd. Although we hope you find this book helpful, it's not intended to be a direct substitute for consultative advice with a healthcare professional, nor do we give any assurance about its effectiveness in a particular case. Accordingly, neither we nor the author shall be held liable for any loss or damages arising from its use.

Index

Note: Page references in *italics* denote figures.

For Product Safety Concerns and Information please contact our EU
representative GPSR@taylorandfrancis.com
Taylor & Francis Verlag GmbH, Kaufingerstraße 24, 80331 München, Germany